PREPARING TO PRAY

Pat Collins CM

Preparing to Pray

101 REFLECTIONS ON SCRIPTURE

the columba press

First published in 2004 by
the columba press
55A Spruce Avenue, Stillorgan Industrial Park,
Blackrock, Co Dublin

Cover by Bill Bolger
Origination by The Columba Press
Printed in Ireland by ColourBooks Ltd, Dublin

ISBN 1 85607 379 3

Contents

Foreword

When you think about Jesus, do you think of him as someone who is forever busy? So many of the gospel stories portray Jesus attending to the legions of people who press him for immediate care: you watch him responding to screams and cries for help and you worry as he risks his life confronting religious authorities about the way they ignore the last and the least and the lost. Wherever Jesus goes, he seems to be followed by an emergency-ward on the move. He is portrayed as the attentive one, the one who is there, the one who notices, the one who listens, the one who reaches out.

Throughout the drama of the public ministry, Jesus seems always on the move: wherever he goes, his presence is communicated through active verbs as he makes things happen. He initiates change, and what he does and says make for new possibility. Sometimes you wonder if he ever sleeps beyond catching forty winks in the boat. Even then, you remember, he is interrupted ...

Yet, in spite of all this energetic drama, so much of Jesus' ministry is rooted in quiet time; out of silence he shares his reflections about God, about the kingdom, and about how we live our lives. He communicates himself as a deeply reflective person, someone who has taken serious time to think about what is important in life, someone who has taken the measure of what really matters, someone who dedicates himself to sharing his insights with others. He is no lonely philosopher; he is a supremely gifted communicator.

There is no paragraph in the gospels where Jesus is portrayed as being alone. He is mentioned, in passing sentences, as escaping from the crowds to be alone in prayer, but the evangelists do not develop stories about this. They have him onstage, teaching, preaching, healing, etc. Yet we guess at the untold stories that happen offstage, the times Jesus needs to be alone, to pray, to think, to assess, to prepare, to be ready for the challenges of his ministry. What Jesus does and says emerges from his own profound prayerful reflections: we are not admitted to this private world in the gospels, but we know it sits quietly behind all the stories about him.

What I especially like about this book, *Preparing to Pray*, is that it emerges as the fruit of extensive private reflection; it is supported by a life of prayer and attentiveness; it comes from a man who has generously shared his thinking and ministry with many people. Fr Pat Collins is a very active priest, but that activity is rooted in a private world that is not seen onstage; it is anchored in personal time dedicated to prayerful reflection on the scriptures.

In this book of 101 reflections, Fr Pat shares the fruit of his reflective time and learning. The range of topics is wide and contemporary, from 'Asylum Seekers' to 'Why go to Confession?' The articles are packed with stories and sharp observation and insights; they are highly readable and provide moments of quiet biblical reflection amidst the bustle of a busy world. They were originally written as a 600-word column for *The Irish Catholic*: they are now gathered together in one volume, providing the reader with a little treasury of meditation.

So many people live busy lives, with little time to pause, reflect, and take stock. This book is an invitation to pause in the company of an experienced pastor and listen to a lively companion share a thought for the day. One reflection is brief enough to use as a daily meditation and sharp enough to keep you going for a week!

Denis McBride CSSR

Introduction

Following all the celebrations associated with the Jubilee that commemorated the passing of two thousand years of Christianity, Pope John Paul II published an encyclical entitled *Novo Millennio Inuente* (2001). It assessed what had happened during the year 2000 and looked forward to the future. Speaking of the importance of a scripture-based spirituality John Paul said in par 39, 'There is no doubt that the primacy of holiness and prayer is inconceivable without a renewed *listening to the word of God.*' Then he went on to make a number of points to do with the renewal of biblical spirituality. He began by saying: 'Ever since the Second Vatican Council underlined the pre-eminent role of the word of God in the life of the church, great progress has certainly been made in devout listening to sacred scripture and attentive study of it.' The Pontiff then proceeded to cite four instances of how this had come about.

1. Scripture in Public Worship

He noted that: 'Scripture has its rightful place of honour in the public prayer of the church.' That is particularly true in the Eucharist, the other sacraments and the Divine Office. Besides using a cycle of numerous scripture readings, many of the prayers they include are based on scripture. Paragraphs 101-141 of the *Catechism of the Catholic Church*, which was published in 1994, are well worth reading because they contain a concise summary of the church's attitude to sacred scripture. They in turn are deeply influenced by *Dei Verbum*, the Dogmatic Decree on Divine Revelation of the Second Vatican Council.

2. Private Use of Scripture

Then the Pope added: 'Individuals and communities now make extensive use of the Bible.' Happily there is a growing number of people who use the scriptures as the basis of their prayer.[1]

---

1. Pat Collins, *Prayer in Practice: A Biblical Approach* (Dublin: Columba, 2000)

Prayer groups, such as charismatic ones, highlight the importance of scripture in their meetings, teachings and sharings.
There are also many Bible groups who, having read and prayerfully reflected on scripture, go on to share their insights with one
another. Sometimes the passage/s they choose are liturgical
ones, such as the readings of the following Sunday's Mass. They
use relatively simple methodologies.[2] I came across the following method in Nigeria where scripture sharing is popular.
Allowing for cultural differences, it can be used by any group re-
gardless of age or education. It consists of the following seven
steps:

1) We invite the Lord to inspire us
Someone prayerfully invites Jesus to help the group.

2) We read the text
Let us open ... chapter such and such, and will someone read
verses ...

3) We pick out specific words and meditate on them
We choose those words or short phrases, read them aloud in
a prayerful way, and keep silence in between

4) We let God speak to us in silence
We keep silence for about five to seven minutes and let the
Spirit lead us into the truth of God's word.

5) We share what we have heard in our hearts
• Which word has touched you personally?
• How can you live out the word of life?

6) We discuss any task which our group is calling us to do
• Report on any task the group may have undertaken
• Which new task could be done?

7) We pray together spontaneously
We end with a prayer or hymn which all know by heart.

This method of scripture sharing also includes the following
evaluation steps:
• Was there a spirit of prayer?
• Was there anything which disturbed or even destroyed the
spirit of prayer?
• Did everybody find the text before it was read?

---

2. Pat Collins, 'Reading and Praying the Scriptures,' *The Broken Image:
Reflections on Spirituality and Culture* (Dublin: Columba, 2002).

- Did we allow a time of silence in between the words or phrases which we picked out?
- Did we read them aloud in a prayerful way?
- Was the time of silence too short or too long?
- Was there real personal sharing or preaching down to others?
- Did we allow the Spirit to guide our discussions or tasks?
- Did we allow enough time for everybody to pray spontaneously?
- What did our facilitator do well?
- How could he or she improve in the future?

3. SCRIPTURE STUDY HELPS AVOID FUNDAMENTALISM

Pope John Paul also observed with approval that: 'Among lay people there are many who devote themselves to scripture with the valuable help of theological and biblical studies.' There are a number of theological colleges and institutes which offer courses on scripture to interested people, whether clerical, religious or lay. Besides these, there are many excellent books on scripture available in the religious bookshops. Happily an increasing number of them have been written by Irish authors. Books on the Bible range from simple introductions, to more learned tomes. At the more scholarly end of the spectrum is the excellent *New Jerome Biblical Commentary*. Besides containing many informative essays on biblical subjects, it contains verse by verse commentaries on each of the books of the Bible. I would also recommend the books of Raymond Brown, especially his *Introduction to the New Testament* and *Responses to 101 Questions on the Bible*.

It is important to state that Catholics are not fundamentalists. We don't interpret the Bible in a literal, non-historical way. Rather, we study the circumstances in which its different books were composed in order to discover the intentions and inspired teaching of its different authors. That is why Bible study is so important. Pope John Paul II has said: 'Attention must be given to the literary forms of the various biblical books in order to determine the intentions of the sacred writers. And it is most helpful, at times crucial, to be aware of the personal situation of the biblical writer, of the circumstances of culture, time, language, etc., which influenced the way the message was presented ... In this way, it is possible to avoid a narrow fundamentalism which distorts the whole truth.'[3]

In saying this, the Holy Father was echoing the teaching of *The Dogmatic Constitution on Divine Revelation*, par 12. It states: 'Since God speaks in sacred scripture through men in human fashion, the interpreter of sacred scripture, in order to see clearly what God wanted to communicate to us, should carefully investigate what meaning the sacred writers really intended, and what God wanted to manifest by means of their words.' The document goes on to say that to appreciate the intention of the sacred writers:

1. Attention must be paid to the literary forms of the scripture.
2. The customary modes of expression at the time of writing.
3. The content and unity of the whole of scripture has to be taken into consideration.
4. Account too must be taken of the harmony between different elements of the faith.
5. All interpretations of scripture must ultimately be subject to the judgement of the church

When he declared St Thérèse a Doctor of the Church, Pope John Paul II commended her for her interest in the true meaning of the scriptures: 'By her loving concentration on scripture – she even wanted to learn Hebrew and Greek to understand better the spirit and letter of the sacred books – she showed the importance of the biblical sources in the spiritual life, she emphasised the originality and freshness of the gospel, she cultivated with moderation the spiritual exegesis of the word of God in both the Old and New Testaments.'[4] Speaking about her prayer life Thérèse testified: 'It is the Bible I use mainly; everything I need for my soul is there.'[5]

By using the *Amplified Bible* translation, which tries to convey the nuances of meaning contained in the original Hebrew or Greek versions of scripture, together with reputable commen-

3. Address to World Catholic Federation for the Biblical Apostolate (1986).
4. *Divini Amoris Scientia*, (1997) par 9.
5. Christopher O Mahoney (Ed.) *St Thérèse of Lisieux by Those who Knew Her* (Dublin: Veritas, 2001), 39.

taries such as the one already mentioned, our understanding of what the sacred writers intended to say, can deepen and grow in the way recommended by the Council Fathers. One could also attend a scripture course. Many dioceses and parishes arrange such courses during the year. If none was available, one might ask a priest, religious or competent lay person to organise such a course locally. I also know of groups of lay men and women who have Bible studies in their homes on a regular basis. They use simple, printed resource methods and materials in order to do so.

In my experience many people find scripture study unsettling, for a time, because it challenges many of their naïve preconceptions. But after a while, it throws an exciting new light on the meaning and implications of the sacred text.

4. SCRIPTURE AND EVANGELISATION

Finally, the Pontiff notes: 'But it is above all the work of evangelisation and catechesis which is drawing new life from attentiveness to the word of God.' This would be particularly obvious in the basic evangelisation approaches of RCIA, Alpha Courses, Life in the Spirit Seminars, Cursillio weekends, and Power to Change programmes. Without exception, they are all scripture based.

TWO RECOMMENDATIONS

In *Nuovo Millennio Inuente* the Pope goes on to make two recommendations. He begins by saying: 'Dear brothers and sisters, this development needs to be consolidated and deepened, also by making sure that every family has a Bible.' This is an important point. I firmly believe that there will be no genuine renewal in the Catholic Church unless and until large numbers of us read, reflect upon, and pray the scriptures on a regular basis. That raises the question, what Bible should families buy? A number of points can be made in this regard.

a) Choosing a Bible

Firstly, there are Catholic and Protestant Bibles. The difference between the two is the fact that Catholic Bibles have more Old

Testament books in them, such as Tobit, Ecclesiasticus, and 1 and 2 Maccabees. Catholics refer to these books as Deutero-canonical, i.e. having been included in the canon at a second (*deutero*) phase – through their adoption as inspired by the Greek-speaking early Christian Church. Some of the more scholarly translations will have lots of additional material, such as introductions to each of the books, learned footnotes that give illuminating information about particular verses, and possibly cross references in the margins which indicate where related verses can be found elsewhere in the Bible.

Secondly, there are literal translations that try to keep as close to the original meaning of the Hebrew or Greek as possible. Accurate Catholic translations of this kind would be *The New Jerusalem Bible, The New Revised Standard Version* (Catholic edition) and *The New American Bible*. Then there are paraphrase translations of the Bible. While they are not as accurate as the literal translations, they try to get the meaning of the text across in a modern, intelligible way. Notable among these are *The Good News Bible* (Catholic edition) and *The Living Bible*. I suspect that many Catholic families would find it easier to read a paraphrase than a literal translation.

Besides using Bibles, many modern day Christians, Catholics and Protestants alike, use other types of scripture books as aids to prayerful reflection. A well known example is *Daily Light*. It contains a thematic sequence of scripture verses, taken from the Old and New Testaments, for every morning and evening of the year. There is a shorter, pocket-sized version, which contains a selection of thematic verses for every day of the year. Those who use either version, on a regular basis, find that the Lord often speaks to them through the theme for that day, such as trusting God no matter what happens, the fruits of the Spirit etc. I find that the *Daily Light* selections often kick start my prayer time. If you decide to buy a copy, check what translation is used. The *King James Version* is old fashioned and hard to read. You would be well advised to try the *New International Version*; it is accurate and intelligible.

b) Lectio Divina
The Holy Father concludes his paragraph on listening to the

word of God with a second recommendation. He says: 'It is especially necessary that listening to the word of God should become a life-giving encounter, in the ancient and ever valid tradition of *lectio divina*, which draws from the biblical text the living word which questions, directs and shapes our lives.' The best known means of paying attention to God's word in the scriptures is the Benedictine Method. It is known as the *lectio divina*, or sacred reading, which Pope John Paul refers to. It's a personal or communal reading of a scripture passage of any length, received as the Word of God, which through the impulse of the Holy Spirit leads to meditation, prayer and contemplation. There are many excellent articles, pamphlets and books available on this topic.[6] Guigo the Carthusian described its overall purpose in a twelfth-century treatise entitled the *Scala Claustralium*, when he wrote: 'Seek in reading and you will find in meditating; knock in prayer and it will be opened to you in contemplation.' *Lectio divina* consists of the following steps:

1. Kiss the Bible as a sign of reverence for God's inspired word.
2. Before engaging in the *lectio divina*, we ask the Lord to bless our prayer time. An Orthodox prayer says:
   Almighty, everlasting God, whose word is a lamp for my feet and a light on my way: open and enlighten my mind, that I may understand your word clearly and accurately. Mould my life according to it, in order that I may never displease you. I ask this through Jesus Christ our Lord. Amen.
3. Choose the passage that you intend to read, e.g. the liturgical reading of that day or the following Sunday.
4. Read the passage slowly two or three times. St Anselm wrote: 'The scriptures are not to be read in a noisy situation, but where things are quiet, not superficially and in a rush, but a little at a time.' It is a good idea to read the passage out tence or a word catches your attention in a special way.
5. Reflect on the meaning of these outstanding verses. As the Lord says: 'Pay attention to my words, listen carefully to my utterances. I say, do not let them out of your sight, keep them

6. Cf Michael de Verteuil, *Your Word is a Light for My Steps: Lectio Divina* (Dublin: Veritas, 1997); Mario Masini, *Lectio Divina* (New York: Alba House, 1998).

deep in your heart. They are life to those who grasp them, health for the entire body' (Prov 4:20-23). There are two ways of carrying out this advice:

a) If you are reflecting on a doctrinal point, e.g. from the letters of St Paul, it can be helpful if you repeat a chosen word or sentence over and over again, while letting its meaning sink into the heart. It is rather like sucking a sweet. You let it dissolve in order to savour its taste and flavour.

b) If you are reflecting on a scriptural story or parable, e.g. one from the gospels, it can be helpful to imagine the incident as if it were a video. See the scene and the characters who are involved; you may choose to be one of them, e.g. an onlooker in the crowd when Jesus is healing a blind man. Hear what is said. You may want to augment the dialogue in the text with some of your own additions. Notice what the characters do. Sense in an empathic way what the people in the incident feel, try especially to sense in an understanding way what Jesus feels, and also try to become aware of your own emotional reaction to the story.

6. Pray from the heart, allowing rational reflection to express itself in the form of an affective conversation with the Lord. St Vincent de Paul once wrote: 'The soul is like a sailboat equipped with oars. The oars are not used unless the wind fails, and then progress isn't as rapid or as pleasant as when the ship is moving along under a fair breeze. Similarly, we have need of reflection in prayer when special assistance from the Holy Spirit is forthcoming, but when the heavenly breeze blows upon the heart, we must yield ourselves to its influence.' We do this when we tell the Lord about our feelings such as love, joy, gratitude, sorrow, desire and the like, which were evoked by reflection on the text. In this regard, St Benedict said: 'Let the prayer be brief and pure.' Once distractions occur go back to reading and reflecting, in the way described, until you can pray again.

7. Contemplate by being still and resting in the Lord. Reflection and prayerful self-disclosure can give way to a sense of union with the revealed presence and purposes of Christ. It occurs when the word of God which is objectively true upon the page leaps into the heart with subjective meaning and

relevance. Scripture speaks of the kind of revelation involved in a number of texts such as: 'Call to me and I will answer you and tell you great and unsearchable things you do not know' (Jer 33:3), and 'From now on I will tell you of new things, of hidden things unknown to you. They are created now, and not long ago; you have not heard of them before today. So you cannot say, "Yes, I knew of them." You have neither heard nor understood; from of old your ear has not been open' (Is 48:6-8). Speaking of this kind of contemplation, St Vincent de Paul remarked: 'It is not the result of human teaching. It is not attainable by human effort, and it is not bestowed on everyone ... In this state of quiet, the soul finds itself suddenly filled with spiritual illuminations and holy affections.' This kind of contemplation usually has a transforming effect (cf 2 Cor 3:18).

Firstly, the contemplative awareness of divine things, 'vitally renews the following of Christ because it leads to an experiential knowledge of him.'[7] Secondly, it results in what one Vatican document referred to as 'theosis' or divinisation.[8] In *Novo Millennio Inuente*, Pope John Paul refers, in moving terms, to the kind of inner transformation that results from contemplating the face of Christ. In par 23 he writes: '"Your face, O Lord, I seek" (Ps 27:8). The ancient longing of the Psalmist could receive no fulfilment greater and more surprising than the contemplation of the face of Christ. God has truly blessed us in him and has made "his face to shine upon us" (Ps 67:1). At the same time, God and man that he is, he reveals to us also the true face of man, "fully revealing man to man himself". Jesus is "the new man" (cf Eph 4:24; Col 3:10) who calls redeemed humanity to share in his divine life. The mystery of the Incarnation lays the foundations for an anthropology which, reaching beyond its own limitations and contradictions, moves towards God himself, indeed towards the goal of "divinisation". This occurs through the grafting of the redeemed on to Christ and their admission into the intimacy of the Trinitarian life.'

7. Par 30, *The Contemplative Dimension of Religious Life*, 1981.
8. Par 3.5 *Jesus Christ Bearer of the Water of Life: A Christian Reflection on the New Age*, 2003.

8. Action. As a result of prayer we begin to see Jesus more clearly
    and to love him more dearly. This leads to a desire to follow
    him more nearly in everyday life. It is good to make a resolu-
    tion that flows from the scriptural reflection and prayer. St
    Vincent de Paul says that such a resolution should be single,
    precise, definite and attainable. As Jesus observed: 'The seed
    on good soil stands for those with a noble and good heart,
    who hear the word, retain it, and by persevering produce a
    crop' (Lk 8:15).

CONCLUSION

I have been reading and praying the scriptures for many years
now. When David Quinn, the editor of *The Irish Catholic*, invited
me to write a weekly, 600-word, scripture reflection for the
paper I had mixed feelings. I was happy to be asked, and daunted
at the prospect of having to produce a column, relentlessly,
every week. David explained that he didn't want scholarly articles,
but rather well informed reflections, the kind that are rooted in
prayer and lead to prayer. I thought about the prospective task,
and eventually said yes, believing that it was a God sent opportunity to do something really worthwhile. I set to work, and to my
surprise found that the task was easier than I had first imagined.
In fact, it turned out to be one of the most enjoyable projects I
have undertaken in a long time. The column has been running
for about two years now. Incidentally, thanks to the generosity
of *The Irish Catholic*, many of the reflections have also been available in the spirituality section of The Irish Vincentians' website
www.vincentians.ie

It is my hope that *Preparing to Pray: 101 Reflections on Scripture*
will be used as a companion volume to my *Prayer in Practice: A
Biblical Approach* (Dublin: Columba, 2000) by acting as a guideline to how one might carry out steps one and two of *lectio divina*,
i.e. of reading and reflecting on the word of God. If I may presume to say something about this. There is a danger that you
may read the reflections quickly with your objective, rational
understanding only. That would be a pity. St Ignatius of Loyola
once wisely observed: 'It is not knowing much, but realising and
relishing things interiorly, that contents and satisfies the soul.'[9]
It is my hope that you will chew and digest what is shared in the

101 scripture reflections. They may contain more spiritual meaning than is apparent at first. Hopefully they will help you to move on to steps three and four of *lectio divina*, of praying to, and contemplating the God of the word. As John Paul II assures us in *Novo Millennio Inuente*, this kind of spiritual exercise will do two things:

a) Challenges worldly attitudes

Firstly, the living word of God questions our individual and collective lives. It is useful, in the words of 2 Tim 3:16, 'for refuting error, for guiding people's lives, and teaching them to be upright'. In doing this it challenges many of our worldly preoccupations, values, attitudes, attachments and behaviours.

b) Scripture gives guidance

Secondly, the Pope says that the living word of God will 'direct and shape the lives' of those who, like Mary the mother of Jesus, ponder the meaning of God's inspired word in a prayerful way. As Ps 119:105 says: 'Your word is a lamp for my feet, a light for my path.' St Paul observed: 'All of us, gazing with unveiled face on the glory of the Lord are being transformed into the same image from glory to glory, as from the Lord who is the Spirit' (2 Cor 3:18). The primary way in which we gaze on the Lord's glory is by reading and praying the scriptures. As we contemplate the word of God, and through it, the God of the word, they can have a transforming effect upon us. Bit by bit we begin to reflect the One whose glory we already dimly behold as in a mirror (cf 1 Cor 13:12).

c) Scripture prepares us for mission

In par 65 of his post-synodal letter, *Ecclesia in Europa* (2003), Pope John Paul summarises many of the points already made, when he writes: 'Church in Europe, enter the new millennium with the Book of the Gospels! May every member of the faithful hear the Council's plea to learn 'the surpassing knowledge of Jesus Christ' (Phil 3:8) by frequent reading of the divine scriptures. "Ignorance of the scriptures is ignorance of Christ." May

---

9. *The Spiritual Exercises*, par 2.

the Holy Bible continue to be a treasure for the church and for every Christian: in the careful study of God's word we will daily find nourishment and strength to carry out our mission.

Let us take up this book! Let us receive it from the Lord who continually offers it to us through his church (cf Rev 10:8). Let us devour it (cf Rev 10:9), so that it can become our very life. Let us savour it deeply: it will make demands of us, but it will give us joy because it is sweet as honey (cf Rev 10:9-10). Filled with hope, we will be able to share it with every man and woman whom we encounter on our way.'

Finally, the aftermath of Jesus' cure of the ten lepers indicates that he appreciated the expression of heartfelt gratitude (cf Lk 17:12-19). I want to take this opportunity of thanking Denis Mc Bride, a well known Redemptorist scripture scholar, lecturer and author, for writing the foreword. I also want to express my gratitude to David Quinn of *The Irish Catholic*, for his encouragement and understanding, and Seán O Boyle of Columba Press for his loyalty and co-operation over the years. Without their differing contributions, this book would not have been written.

1 Book of Books

Pope John Paul II said some time ago: 'In order to recognise who Christ truly is, Christians should turn with renewed interest to the bible, 'whether it be through the liturgy, rich in the divine word, or through devotional reading, or through instructions suitable for the purpose and other aids.' I'm firmly persuaded that there will be no genuine, long lasting renewal in the contemporary church unless it is rooted in and nourished by the word of God.

All the books of the Old Testament point to Christ and find their fulfillment in him. Jesus himself made this clear to the two disciples on the road to Emmaus. Having poured out their sorrows to their companion, 'Jesus replied: "You foolish men! So slow to believe the full message of the prophets! Was it not ordained that the Christ should suffer and so enter his glory?" Then starting with Moses and going through all the prophets he explained to them the passages throughout the scriptures that were about himself' (Lk 24:25-28).

The gospels record the words and actions of Jesus himself. They are like so many panes in the stained glass window of his humanity. When they are illuminated by the Spirit and contemplated with the eyes of faith, they can become a unique source of revelation. Through them we begin to see what God is like. As Jesus said: 'To have seen me is to have seen the Father' (Jn 14:9). The remaining books of the New Testament record the impact and implications of Christ for the first Christians.

The New Testament authors often speak about the importance of God's word. 'All scripture is inspired by God … it is something alive and active … it is the sword of the Spirit … it can judge the secret thoughts and emotions of the heart … and is useful for teaching truth, rebuking error, correcting faults, and giving instruction for living' (2 Tim 3:1; Heb 4:12; Eph 6:7; 2 Tim 3:1). No wonder St Jerome once wrote: 'The person who doesn't know the scriptures doesn't know Jesus Christ.'

Vatican II also stressed the fundamental importance of scripture. In the *Dogmatic Constitution on Divine Revelation* par 11, we read: 'the books of scripture must be acknowledged as teaching firmly, faithfully and without error that truth which God wanted put into the sacred writings for the sake of our salvation.' Catholics believe that the Holy Spirit can lead the individual believer into the truth of God's word. As a verse of a hymn in the Divine Office reads:

In the scriptures by the Spirit,
may we see the Saviour's face,
hear his word and heed his calling,
know his will and grow in grace.'

The church encourages the faithful to develop a scripture-based spirituality. For example, in par 133 of *The Catechism of the Catholic Church* we read: 'The church forcefully and specifically exhorts all the Christian faithful ... to learn the surpassing knowledge of Jesus Christ, by frequent reading of the scriptures.' To do this, we ponder them in a prayerful way while asking two key questions. What is God saying to me through the verses I have read, and how does it relate to the circumstances of my life and the lives of the people around me?

Francis Bacon once wrote: 'Some books are to be tasted, others to be swallowed and some few to be chewed and digested.' Needless to say, the bible is pre-eminent among the latter.

2 Scripture and Conversion

An interesting passage in Acts 8:26-40 describes both the geo-graphical and spiritual journey of an Ethiopian eunuch who was an official in the court of queen Candece. Apparently, the word Ethiopia may have originally meant black. It is possible that this Negro was from some exotic region of Africa, such as the Sudan or Egypt. Wherever he was from, he had a sincere desire to know the Lord. Why else would he have gone so far to worship in Jerusalem? The Lord has promised that such longings will never be in vain: 'You will call upon me and come and pray to me, and I will listen to you. You will seek me and find me when you seek me with all your heart' (Jer 29:12-14).

Apparently he travelled down a deserted, desert road. It was the outward symbol of his own inner loneliness and aridity. He was attentively reading Is 53:7-8. As he did so, Philip was led by an angel to go down that same road and to make contact. In Greek the word angel literally means messenger of the Lord. As Heb 13:2 advised: 'Do not forget to entertain strangers, for by so doing some people have entertained angels without knowing it.' It may be that some member of the Christian community had given Philip a prophetic word of guidance. He in turn became the eunuch's God-appointed angel.

We are told that he ran up to the chariot and heard the man reading. He asked if he understood the passage. 'How can I,' he said, 'unless someone explains it to me?' On the church's behalf Philip proceeded to tell him that it was a prophetic anticipation of the future coming of the Suffering Servant. Then he shared the good news about Jesus, the Son of God, who had died and risen in order that our sins might be forgiven. He would also have told him how the risen Lord pours out the Holy Spirit on those who are baptised, thereby enabling them to grasp how wide and long and high and deep is the unrestricted and uncon-ditional love of God, that surpasses human understanding, so that he might be filled with the presence of God.

I suspect that the eunuch was deeply moved when Philip told him about Jesus; how he had suffered great injustice at the hands of the Jewish and Roman authorities, had been humiliated in public, and died without heirs. He could identify with the Lord. He had suffered the childhood injustice of involuntary castration. As a result of his appearance and high pitched voice he had often endured ridicule, and because of his infertility he could have no children. He could see that Jesus, as God's son, had completely identified with his suffering and shame as an outsider. This was his moment of revelation, of spiritual awakening. Inwardly, he felt accepted and loved by Jesus.

His response was instantaneous and wholehearted. Not only did he believe in the Good News, he immediately asked to be baptised. 'Then both Philip and the eunuch went down into the water and Philip baptised him.' At last, his search was over. He felt the joy of ultimate belonging. Then as mysteriously as he had appeared, Philip disappeared. He had been effective as a witness to Christ because, from first to last, he had been led by the Spirit. Instead of preaching or imposing his agenda, he had listened sensitively to the eunuch and responded to his questions. As a model evangelist, he was able, in this way, to satisfy the man's God-prompted desire to know God.

3 Needs and Priorities

Many years ago I attended a conference for priests. At one point, a lay man addressed us. He said something that I have never forgotten. 'In the future, the priest or lay person, who concentrates on satisfying urgent needs to the exclusion of Christian priorities will contribute, by default, to the demise of the church.' It is a striking comment. And I think that it is true.

There is a passage in Mk 1:32-38 which illustrates it. Late one evening, Jesus arrived in a village after sunset. News of his coming spread quickly, and many sick and oppressed people were brought to him. We are told that 'Jesus healed many who had various diseases. He also drove out many demons.' Besides providing evidence of the powerful effectiveness of his ministry, this verse is interesting, because the word 'many' may imply that, for one reason or another, Jesus didn't heal and deliver all who were brought to him. Perhaps it was due to their unbelief.

Quickly the scene changes. 'Very early in the morning, while it was still dark, Jesus got up, left the house and went off to a solitary place, where he prayed.' As a man of prayer, he often went off on his own to commune with his Father. Like Moses of old, he would enter the tent of his heart, the cloud of Spirit would cover him, and he would pour out his feelings, reactions and desires to God. Then Yahweh would speak to him face to face as a man does with his friend (cf Ex 33:11). Presumably, during this time, Jesus discerned, precisely, how his Father wanted him to carry out his mission of bringing the good news to the poor.

Then the scene changes again. We are told that: 'Simon and his companions went to look for him, and when they found him, they exclaimed: "Everyone is looking for you!"' Because of his magnetic personality, his authoritative teaching, and deeds of power, it is not surprising that crowds of people were always longing to meet Jesus. After all, their needs were very real and pressing. Presumably, as soon as word spread about the healings and exorcisms he had performed the previous evening, lots more people suffering from diseases, handicaps, and spiritual

problems had gathered in the village square hoping for his healing and liberating touch.

In spite of his unquestionable compassion, Jesus replied: 'Let
us go somewhere else – to the nearby villages – so I can preach
there also. That is why I have come.' In other words, he seemed
to be saying, 'I know that there is an endless succession of urgent needs. But in the name of the evangelical priorities God has
given me, sadly, I will have to resist the pull of these very genuine requests.'

Members of today's church, bishops, priests and lay people,
have a lot to learn from this passage. As in New Testament
times, we are faced by an unending number of pressing problems. Many of us will suffer from burnout if we try to satisfy all
of them. Like Jesus we need to have a clear and conscious sense
of what our core mission is. Then, after prayerful discernment,
we need to focus our efforts on achieving our goals. Needless to
say, we can try, with God's help, to satisfy people's legitimate
needs in so far as they fit in with our evangelistic priorities and
abilities. As Jesus once assured his disciples: 'Seek first God's
kingdom and his righteousness, and all these things will be
given to you as well' (Mt 6:33).

4 The Promises of God

Like most Catholics, I love the scripture passages that refer to Mary. There are not too many of them, so that makes the ones we have all the more precious. The gospel account of the visitation in Lk 1:39-56 is one of my favourites. It is positively Pentecostal in so far as Elizabeth and Mary are both filled with the Holy Spirit. They speak with joy in an inspired and inspiring way. In this reflection I want to focus on something important Elizabeth said to her cousin.

If we were to ask those who have devotion to Mary, why she is blessed, I think we would get a great variety of answers. While their responses would probably be true, it is interesting to note what God says through the prophetic lips of Elizabeth: 'Blessed is she who has believed that what the Lord has said to her will be accomplished!' In other words, Mary is blessed, principally, because of her trust in the God of the promises and in the promises of God.

When Gabriel appeared to Mary he promised her that she would become the mother of the Messiah, through the overshadowing of the Holy Spirit, to whom nothing was impossible. In response, Mary had said: 'May it be to me as you have said' (Lk 1:38). Like all the great heroes of faith in the Old Testament, instead of relying on her limited, rational understanding, Mary trusted in God with all her heart. She knew that the Lord had said: 'As the rain and the snow come down from heaven, and do not return to it without watering the earth and making it bud and flourish, so that it yields seed for the sower and bread for the eater, so is my word that goes out from my mouth: It will not return to me empty, but will accomplish what I desire and achieve the purpose for which I sent it' (Is 55:10-11).

Abraham, like Mary, was outstanding for his unwavering trust in God. As St Paul commented: 'Without weakening in his faith, he faced the fact that his body was as good as dead – since he was about a hundred years old – and that Sarah's womb was also dead. Yet he did not waver through unbelief regarding the promise of God, but was strengthened in his faith and gave glory to God, being fully persuaded that God had power to do what he had promised' (Rom 4:19-21). In due course his trust was vindicated when Isaac was born. Mary is our mother in faith. Like Abraham, she believed that God would do what the angel said. Her unwavering trust was rewarded when Jesus was born.

If, like Mary, we want to live by faith, we need to take shelter under the umbrella of God's promises in all the events of our lives. The divine undertakings cover all the situations we have to face in our everyday lives. When you come across them in your bible, whether to do with salvation, God's willingness to answer prayer, or to give us eternal life, why not underline them? Many years ago, I wrote the following verse. I know it's not exactly Shakespearian, but it tries to express my personal conviction.

God is as good as his word.
You know that his promise is true.
Whatever you ask for in his name,
The same shall be done for you.

In the beautiful words of the Hail Holy Queen we can say, 'Pray for us, most holy Mother of God, that we may be made worthy of the promises of Christ.'

5 Claiming the Promises

Scripture assures us that, 'Nothing is impossible to God' (Lk 1:37). It also assures us that we can place firm confidence in the many promises of God in the scriptures because 'He who has promised is faithful' (Heb 10:23).

That said, many people become disillusioned when God doesn't seem to keep the divine word. For example, a pensioner may pray repeatedly that a young mother will recover from cancer, but nothing seems to happen. No wonder he asks, 'Why did the Lord ignore my pleas, after all he has promised to answer our prayers?' There is no simple answer. Sometimes we are told, 'God has answered your prayer, but not in the way you expected' or 'who has known the mind of the Lord?' While there is some truth in both responses, neither is fully convincing. There is another possibility.

In the Old Testament, the promises of God are usually associated with conditions. For instance, over the thirty years of the troubles in Northern Ireland, many people focused on a powerful verse in 2 Chr 7:14. In it the Lord says: 'If my people, who are called by my name, will humble themselves and pray and seek my face and turn from their wicked ways, then will I hear from heaven and will forgive their sin and will heal their land.' Notice that God promises to do three things, to hear, forgive and heal. But those undertakings depend on people's willingness to fulfil four stated conditions. Although nationalists and unionists repeatedly prayed for the conflict to end, did they do so in a spirit of humility? Often they seemed to display an arrogant, self-righteous attitude. Did they always seek God's face? Often they appeared to pursue their own selfish interests, rather than the will of God. Did they turn from their wicked ways? Often they asked for peace while willingly tolerating serious sin in their private lives. No wonder it took so long for their petitions to be answered.

St Paul says: 'All the promises of God find their Yes in Jesus' (2 Cor 1:20). In the gospels the promises of Christ, like the Old Testament ones, are also associated with conditions. For example, many stressful people love the words, 'Come to me, all you who are weary and burdened, and I will give you rest' (Mt 11:28). That's great. But they often overlook the associated conditions in the following verse. 'Take my yoke upon you and learn from me, for I am gentle and humble in heart, and you will find rest for your souls' (Mt 11:29). Apparently, the yoke refers to the law of love. Besides loving others as Christ loves us, we need to do so in a gentle and humble way like him. It is then, and only then that an anxious person will find the inner peace he or she is longing for.

In Mk 11:24 there is another significant promise that applies to all kinds of petitions: 'I tell you, whatever you ask for in prayer, believe that you have received it, and it will be yours.' The condition is right there in the middle. If we are honest about it, while many of us hope that we may receive what we ask for, in the future, how many of us trust, in an unhesitating way, that we are actually receiving what we are asking for, right now, in the present? So when you read the promises of God, be sure to read and observe the small print as well. God won't be able to fulfil them until you do.

6 Self-forgetful Attention

Pause and think about this question for a moment. In the gospels, what is the very first verb used to describe the activity of Jesus? The answer is to be found in a childhood incident when Jesus became separated from Joseph and Mary for three days. Eventually they found him in the temple among the elders. We are told that he was: 'listening to them and asking them questions' (Lk 2:46).

Implicit in the attentive listening of Jesus, was a powerful, single minded desire to acquire divine wisdom. Presumably, he had often heard the scriptures being read in his local synagogue. His visit to the temple could have been prompted by Sir 6:33-37. It says: 'If you love to listen you will gain knowledge, and if you incline your ear you will become wise. Stand in the assembly of the elders. Who is wise? Cleave to him. Be ready to listen ... If you see an intelligent man, visit him early; let your foot wear out his doorstep. The Lord will give insight to your mind, and your desire for wisdom will be granted.' Isn't that just what Jesus did when he spent time in the temple?

In adult life Jesus continued to be a good listener. Instead of paying attention to the elders in the Jerusalem temple, he listened to his heavenly Father in the inner sanctum of his heart, where he would hear him speaking. All Jesus' words and actions were rooted in the revelation of his Father's word. As Jesus himself testified: 'I do nothing on my own, but I speak these things as the Father instructed me' (Jn 8:28), and 'The Son can only do what he sees the Father doing: and whatever the Father does, the Son does too' (Jn 5:19). So, every word and action of Jesus was the fruit of his listening.

His ministry was characterised by obedience to his Father. It is interesting to note that the word in English is derived from the Latin meaning 'to listen thoroughly'. In other words, the obedience of Jesus should be seen as the expression of his attentive listening to God his beloved Father. So when scripture says that he: 'humbled himself and became obedient to death' (Phil 2:3), it is saying that right up to the end, Jesus remained open and re-

ceptive to the word of his loving Father. This he freely carried
out as a matter of loving conviction.

It is obvious from the gospels, that Jesus not only listened to
his Father, he also listened in an empathic, self-forgetful way to
the verbal and non-verbal disclosures of the needy people he
met. For example in Mk 10:46-52, Bartimaeus, a blind man asked
Jesus for help. Instead of presuming to know what was best for
him, Jesus asked with exquisite sensitivity: 'What do you want
me to do for you?' He listened attentively to the man's reply,
and responded accordingly. When the Samaritan woman spoke
to him at Jacob's well (cf Jn 4:5-44), he listened attentively to her
words and body-language. As a result, he had an intimate understanding of her spiritual aspirations.

In the light of these points it could be said, with some justification, that listening is the foundation stone of Christian spirituality. It is not surprising, therefore, that Protestant theologian,
Dietrich Bonhoeffer, once wrote: 'Many people are looking for
an ear that will listen. They do not find it among Christians, because they are too busy talking when they should be listening.
The person who no longer listens to his or her neighbour will
soon not be listening to God either ... This is the beginning of
spiritual death.'

7 Fear is Not from God

Timothy was one of the first bishops to be ordained by St Paul. Subsequently two letters were written to his young protégé. In the second there is a passage I really like. The writer says: 'I remind you to fan into flame the gift of God, which is in you through the laying on of my hands. For God did not give us a spirit of fear, but a spirit of power, of love and of self-control' (2 Tim 1:6-7).

In the days before central heating, people would light the fire during cold weather. When they got up in the morning it would have stopped burning. But when the surface ashes were removed, dimly glowing embers were often exposed. If someone blew upon them they would begin to glow brightly before bursting into flames. Paul is saying, 'Perhaps you have lost your first fervour. If so, fan it into a flame once again.'

The text implies that the root cause for such a loss of spiritual enthusiasm, is not so much a lack of prayer as a debilitating feeling of anxiety and fear. It is my own belief that these are the most deep-seated emotional responses of creatures like ourselves, who live in a dangerous and threatening world where we can become the hapless victims of the 'slings and arrows of outrageous fortune' at any time. I also suspect that many of our other negative feelings, such as anger, guilt, resentment and grief, are secretly rooted in a defensive fear of diminishment and loss.

Spiritual writers are agreed that, next to sin, anxious fear is the greatest enemy of the spiritual life. The word 'anxiety' in English, comes from the Latin, meaning 'to choke, to press tightly or to oppress.' Anxious fear makes people to be mistrustful and defensive in such a way that they become narrow minded and cowardly. Consequently they are less open and receptive to the surprises and invitations of the Spirit. Knowing this to be true, St Paul says to Timothy that the Spirit he received in the sacraments of baptism and confirmation and later in his ordination, was not a spirit of anxious fear.

It seems to me that this is a very important point as far as the discernment of spirits is concerned. Whenever one is faced with an important choice, such as telling a relative or friend that we think he is drinking too much; standing up for our Christian convictions when they are ridiculed at work; or deciding to undertake some demanding task, it is important to notice whether one's decision, to act or not to act, is being motivated by fear. For any conscientious Christian who wants to be guided by the Spirit, it is important to recognise that our feelings of anxiety and fear, whether they are prompted by our own insecurity, or the illusions and false inspirations of the devil, do not come from the Spirit of God.

So if we notice that anxious fear is prompting us to avoid risks, by playing safe, we need to acknowledge those feelings. Then we can turn to the Lord, to ask him for the power to courageously do what is right. As St Paul assures us, the Holy Spirit, will strengthen us inwardly in our innermost selves, thereby giving us the precious gift of self-control. As St Paul said in another place: 'The Lord said to me, "My grace is sufficient for you, for my strength is made perfect in weakness"' (2 Cor 12:9), and 'I can do all things through Christ who strengthens me' (Phil 4:13).

8 Peculiar People

As you know there are many English translations of the bible. Among the oldest are the Catholic Douai-Reims Bible (1610) and the Protestant, King James Bible (1611). Fewer and fewer people use them now because of scholarly inaccuracies and the fact that the language they employ is quaint and out of date. Happily, nowadays, there are many accurate and intelligible translations such as the Protestant, *New International Version*, and the Catholic *New Jerusalem Bible*. In this reflection, I want to focus on two similar verses from the King James Version, one from the Old Testament, the other from the New.

In Deut 26:18 we read: 'The Lord hath avouched thee this day to be his peculiar people.' In Titus 2:14 we read, 'Jesus gave himself for us, that he might redeem us from all iniquity, and purify unto himself a peculiar people.' In modern translations the words 'peculiar people' is replaced by phrases such as 'treasured people', 'special possession', 'peculiarly his own'. When I first read these verses many years ago I was really amused by the reference to 'peculiar people'. It seemed to imply that believers who have been chosen and blessed by God are a bit odd and eccentric. I suppose that there are many people in modern society who would concur with this understanding of the word. They would be inclined to agree with Sigmund Freud's view that people of religious faith are peculiar in the sense that they are suffering from an obsessive compulsive neurosis.

When one looks up the meaning of the word 'peculiar' in a dictionary it is very revealing. Apparently it is derived from the Latin *peculium* meaning, 'private property'. In the Roman world there were many slaves who were owned by masters who had bought them as items of property. As a result, slaves had very few rights. However, Roman law stipulated that if an owner wanted to sell one of his slaves, the unfortunate man or woman had a right to hold on to his or her *peculium*, i.e. private possessions he or she was able to acquire. They could not be separated from them, and were legally entitled to bring them to their new domicile.

So when the King James translation refers to 'peculiar people' it is saying that the believers are God's chosen ones, his private possession, so to speak, who cannot be separated from the Lord. Isn't that a wonderfully consoling thought. Nothing can separate us from the unconditional, and unrestricted love of God. As St Paul declared in Rom 8:35-39: 'Who shall separate us from the love of Christ? Shall trouble or hardship or persecution or famine or nakedness or danger or sword? ... No, in all these things we are more than conquerors through him who loved us. For I am convinced that neither death nor life, neither angels nor demons, neither the present nor the future, nor any powers, neither height nor depth, nor anything else in all creation, will be able to separate us from the love of God that is in Christ Jesus our Lord.'

I can recall seeing a poster once, which asked the question, 'If God seems far away, who has moved?' The verses we are reflecting on are saying, although we may separate ourselves from God as a result of our sins, God will never be separated from us. Once chosen, we are forever the adopted children of God, the Lord's precious possession. Odd as it may seem, God the Father never withdraws the divine anointing from his people. So I hope you feel peculiar, because, in God's eyes, you are!

9 Back to Basics

The gospel of Mark recounts the very first words preached by Jesus during his public ministry. They were: 'The time has come,' he said. 'The kingdom of God is near. Repent and believe the good news!' (Mk 1:15). This verse is of foundational importance. Let's begin with the declaration, 'the time has come'. What Jesus is pointing out is that the period of waiting is over, the promised messiah, spoken of by many of the Old Testament prophets, has finally come. Jesus made a similar statement, sometime later in his local synagogue at Nazareth. He read a passage from Is 61:1-2 and concluded by saying: 'Today this scripture is fulfilled in your hearing.'

Jesus, then went on to declare that the kingdom of God was close at hand. This was a key point in his preaching. It was principally addressed to people who were suffering in material and spiritual ways. He knew from personal experience what they had to endure. Taxes were heavy. Famines were frequent. Emigration was high. Roman rule was cruel. Physical and mental diseases were many and incurable. But the principal suffering of the poor was their sense of alienation from God. The religious authorities of the day had told them they were sinners without hope either because they were engaged in unclean professions such as prostitution, tax collecting, robbing, looking after herds, lending money at high interest, or gambling, not paying tithes, neglecting the Sabbath day of rest and ignoring Jewish rules of ritual cleanliness. They were also damned because, through no fault of their own, they were ignorant of the details of the law. Not only were they were they losers in this life, they would also be losers in the next. In Jn 7:49, the Pharisees refer to the people, I have described, as 'the accursed', i.e. those who had no prospect of salvation.

When Jesus said that God's kingdom was near at hand, he was saying that God's reign of unconditional forgiveness and love was breaking into people's lives, free *gratis* and for nothing. They didn't have to earn or deserve it by means of good works. All they had to do was to look into the eyes of God's mercy and love, expecting only mercy and love, and they would receive only mercy and love. When Jesus spoke like this, it probably sounded too good to be true. That is why he performed deeds of power such as healings, exorcisms and miracles. They were the good news in action. When the people experienced the liberating deeds that Jesus performed by means of the Spirit working in and through him, it began to dawn on them, that his message of salvation must be true after all.

Jesus told them how to enter God's kingdom. 'Repent,' he said, 'and believe the good news.' Many people mistakenly think that the word repentance refers principally to a willingness to turn away from sinful attitudes and actions as a precondition for receiving God's merciful love. Not so. The word repentance in Greek literally means 'to think again'. What we have to accept is that God's offer of love does not depend on what we do. Rather it depends completely on what God is doing, by offering us the gift of unconditional mercy and love. Once we accept that truth with our minds, we need to believe it completely with our hearts. Then, having received God's grace, we do try, with its help, to turn away from our sinful behaviour. We do this, not as a means of deserving God's gift, but as a grateful response for the undeserved gift we have already received.

10 Pray Always

On four separate occasions the New Testament tells us to pray continuously. Lk 18:1 we read: 'Then Jesus told his disciples a parable to show them that they should always pray and not give up.' Eph 5:20 says: 'Pray at all times in the Spirit, with all prayer and supplication.' Eph 6:18 echoes this point when it says: 'And pray in the Spirit on all occasions with all kinds of prayers and requests. With this in mind, be alert and always keep on praying for all the saints.' Finally, in 1 Thess 5:18 St Paul gives this succinct injunction 'pray continually'.

Over the centuries there have been many ways of interpreting these verses, such as Cassian's use of a mantra, or the Orthodox Church's use of the Jesus Prayer. Unceasing prayer can be understood as the liturgy of the heart, the praying voice of the Spirit within, who, consciously or unconsciously, aspires to the God beyond, by praying 'Abba Father' (Rom 8:15; Gal 4:6). Unceasing prayer can also be looked at as a form of action, a handing over the fruits of contemplation to others, principally by means of preaching, teaching and good works. St Basil once said: 'This is how to pray continually – not by offering prayer in words, but by joining yourself to God through your whole way of life, so that your life becomes one continuous and uninterrupted prayer.' Unceasing prayer can be understood as ongoing desire to know the person, word and will of God. As St Augustine wrote: 'For desire never ceases to pray even though the tongue be silent. If ever desiring, then ever praying.' Unceasing prayer can also be seen as the permanent state of loving. The Christian life is essentially a loving response to the love of God. So it could be said that to pray is to love God and to love God in the neighbour is to pray.

From a scriptural point of view, however, there is the more down-to-earth notion of persistence in petitionary prayer. In the Old Testament the Hebrew word *tamid* can mean 'at all times' in the sense that an action is repeated on a regular basis. Understood in this sense, the call to unceasing prayer could be interpreted, simply, as a call to faithfulness to regular times of prayer at morning, noon and night.

41

Jesus taught that we should ask, in prayers of petition, for our own needs and, in prayers of intercession, for the needs of others. We should do so in a persistent, confident way. Jesus illustrated what he meant in two of his parables. Firstly there is the story of the friend who comes at midnight and continues to ask for bread until the householder gives it to him (Lk 11:5-9). Secondly there is the account of the importunate widow who keeps pestering the unjust judge who eventually gives her what she wants in order to get her off his back (Lk 18:2-9). In both cases the reluctant friend and the unenthusiastic judge finally give the petitioners what they ask. So Jesus is saying, keep on asking for what you need and you shall receive it from your gracious Father in heaven.

Besides asking God to satisfy our immediate needs, the New Testament encourages us to persist in asking God to hasten the second coming of Jesus at the end of time. For example, when we pray, in the Lord's Prayer, 'give us this day our daily bread' it could be translated to read 'Give us today a foretaste of the heavenly banquet we long for.'

11 Money and Evil

Very few of us can read the bible in the original languages in which it was written. We have to rely on English translations. By and large, these fall into two main groups. Firstly, there are scholarly versions that try to translate the original text as exactly as possible. Secondly, there are popular versions which paraphrase the original text in order to get the meaning across in a way that is intelligible and relevant to the modern reader. If it's accuracy you want, buy a scholarly translation rather than a paraphrase.

However, it is not as simple as that. Scholars themselves sometimes have difficulty translating Hebrew or Greek phrases into English because they could have two possible meanings in the original. I'll give an example, which has often puzzled me. It can be found in 1 Tim 6:10. It is an ancient proverb, which was current in New Testament times, and is often misquoted to read: 'Money is the root of all evil.' The *Revised English Bible*, the *New American Bible*, and the *New Jerusalem Bible* all translate it to read: 'The love of money is the root of all evil,' while, the *New Revised Standard Version*, and the *New International Version* say: 'The love of money is a root of all kinds of evil.' These are all scholarly translations which attempt to be as accurate as possible. They all agree that the love of money is a problem. After all, Jesus warned, 'you cannot serve God and money' (Mt 6:24). In other words, if people have an inordinate love of money, if they suffer from greed and rely on cash rather than God, it will have bad knock-on effects.

However, the translations of the second half of the verse are not agreed about the exact nature of the effect. It seems to me that there is a significant difference between saying that the love of money is a root of all kinds of evil, and saying it is the root of all evil.

From an experiential point of view, I'd be more inclined to accept the first translation. I can see that the love of money is indeed the root cause of many of the evils that beset our world, such as war and pornography, social injustice and global warming. But I find it hard to accept that the love of money is the root of every evil we endure. How could it be the cause of such things as destructive earthquakes, sudden floods, or debilitating diseases and disorders such Alzheimer's, haemophilia, and cerebral palsy? So, from a rational, and practical point of view, I'd incline towards the notion that the love of money is the root cause of many of the world's avoidable evils.

From a Christian point of view we should use money as a means to living a good Christian life, but not as an end in itself. Heb 13:5 says: 'Keep your lives free from the love of money and be content with what you have, because God has said, "Never will I leave you; never will I forsake you."' Rather than trying to accumulate more and more of it, we should be generous by sharing our surplus money with the less well off members of society. As 1 Tim 6:17-19 says: 'Command those who are rich in this present world not to be arrogant nor to put their hope in wealth, which is so uncertain, but to put their hope in God, who richly provides us with everything for our enjoyment. Command them to do good, to be rich in good deeds, and to be generous and willing to share.'

12 Immersed in the Spirit

If I were asked to choose the verse I consider the most important in the New Testament, I would have a few possible contenders in mind. One of them would be Jn 1:33. John had been administering the baptism of repentance. Then, mysteriously, Jesus approached him and asked to be baptised. When he complied, 'John gave this testimony: "I saw the Spirit come down from heaven as a dove and remain on him"' (Jn 1:32). Then he proceeded to say in a prophetic manner: 'The man on whom you see the Spirit come down and remain is he who will baptise with the Holy Spirit.' Commenting on these words, a footnote in *The New Jerusalem Bible* says that, 'this phrase sums up the whole purpose of the Messiah's coming, namely, that humanity might be born again in the Spirit.'

The word baptism is derived from Greek, and literally means, 'to immerse', i.e. to drench, soak, saturate or inundate. Imagine a sponge being plunged into water. When it is squeezed, every bubble of air is expelled. When it is released every pore becomes filled with water. When Jesus was immersed in the waters of the Jordan, it was an outward sign of the fact that inwardly he was being anointed with the Spirit of God. There is reason to believe that this mystical experience was a very significant one in his life. He became consciously aware, as never before, of the infinite love that God the Father was lavishing on him as his Son, the One endowed with every perfection of divinity. As he said from heaven: 'You are my Son, whom I love; with you I am well pleased' (Lk 3:22).

In the light of this outpouring of the Spirit, Jesus realised who he was, and what he was being called to do. He was the Christ, the anointed One, the promised Messiah. He was being called to show to the people, especially the poor, outcasts and sinners, the infinite love God was showing to him. He was to offer it to them in an unconditional, unrestricted way. He would do so by means of his anointed words, and deeds. They would be so many ways of saying to the people: 'As the Father has loved me, so have I loved you' (Jn 15:9).

During his public ministry Jesus had a growing realisation, that while the people might gain a superficial knowledge of God's merciful love, as a result of his ministry, they would only become fully aware of it when they, like him, were baptised in the Spirit. This could only happen after his death, and glorific- ation. He often spoke in a symbolic way about the promised Holy Spirit as water. For example, in Jn 7:37-39 he cried out: 'If anyone is thirsty, let him come to me and drink. Whoever be- lieves in me, as the scripture has said, streams of living water will flow from within him.' By this he meant the Spirit, whom those who believed in him were later to receive. When he died on the cross, a soldier pierced his side with a lance and, symbolic- ally, out flowed the water of the Spirit (Jn 19:34).

Why not pray to be immersed in the Spirit? 'I ask God that with both feet planted firmly on love, I'll be able to take in with all Christians the extravagant dimensions of Christ's love. May I be enabled to reach out and experience its breadth, test its length, plumb its depths and rise to its heights. With the Spirit's help may I live a full life, full in the fullness of God' (cf Eph 3:17-19).

13 The Shield of Faith

Scott Peck, began his bestseller, *The Road Less Travelled*, with the sentence, 'life isn't easy'. How true. Each one of us has to contend with the slings and arrows of outrageous fortune. We have to cope with predictable crises, such as adolescence and the midlife transition, and unpredictable crises such as personal ill-health and bereavement. Besides these difficulties, we can be afflicted by spiritual attacks from the evil one. He can exercise a malevolent influence upon us by means of inward illusions, false inspirations, temptations and oppression, or outward disturbances such as the infestation of a building. As scripture says: 'Our struggle is not against flesh and blood, but against the rulers, against the authorities, against the powers of this dark world and against the spiritual forces of evil in the heavenly realms' (Eph 6:12). St Peter echoed these words when he said: 'Your enemy the devil prowls around like a roaring lion looking for someone to devour' (1 Pet 5:8).

Over the years many people have contacted me to ask how to cope with either the inward or outward assaults of the devil. Scripture gives us a number of helpful pieces of advice such as: 'Be self-controlled and alert ... Resist him, standing firm in the faith' (1 Pt 5:8, 9), and 'Submit yourselves to God. Resist the devil, and he will flee from you' (Jas 4:7). But my favourite is: 'Take up the shield of faith, with which you can extinguish all the flaming arrows of the evil one' (Eph 6:16).

You may have noticed in the film *Gladiator* that Roman soldiers had two types of shield. The one referred to here was the larger of the two. It was oval shaped, four and a half feet high and two and a half feet wide. It consisted of two or three layers of plywood and was covered with painted leather. In the earlier phase of a battle, when the enemy were firing arrows tipped with burning pitch, the soldiers would drench their shields with water, form a tortoise shape, and crouch behind them for protection. St Paul says that the shield of faith will put out all the fiery darts of the evil one, just as the shields of the Roman soldiers would ward off burning arrows. Scripture repeatedly makes it clear that the Lord is our spiritual shield. For example, in Prov 30:5 we read: 'He (God) is a shield to those who take refuge in him' and 'My shield is God Most High' (Ps 7:10).

This is an important assurance. We can deal with all the fiery darts of greed, lust, jealousy, envy, unbelief, resentment etc., by raising the shield of faith. This can be done by saying the holy name of Jesus with faith. In other words, although we do indeed resist the devil, we don't do so directly. Rather we take refuge in him who is greater than our adversary. When asked how she had survived the evils of life in a concentration camp, the late Corrie Ten Boom replied, 'I learned to nestle and not to wrestle.' In other words, when she was confronted by evil from either within or without her personality, she nestled in the Lord through faith instead of wrestling directly with it. As Paul assures us: 'The weapons we fight with are not the weapons of the world. On the contrary, they have divine power to demolish strongholds (i.e. of wrong thinking inspired by the evil one). We demolish arguments and every pretension that sets itself up against the knowledge of God, and we take captive every thought to make it obedient to Christ' (2 Cor 10:4-5).

14 Baptism, Confirmation and the Spirit

If Christians receive the Holy Spirit in baptism and confirmation, in what sense, if any, can we say that as adults they are 'baptised in, or filled with the Spirit'? Theologians point out that while we do receive the Holy Spirit in the sacraments of initiation, it is a sacramental rather than an experiential event. It is like a boy having an inheritance in the bank. The money is there in his name, but it cannot be used until he reaches the age of twenty-one. Then and only then will he be able to do the things he could only dream of doing beforehand. The same can be true of contemporary Christians. They are heirs to all the blessings that Christ experienced. But until they can claim them by faith in the promises of God, and through the release of the Holy Spirit within their personalities, they may have the desire, but they will not have the power to do great things for God.

There is scriptural support for this point of view in the account of the evangelisation of the Samaritans in Acts 8:14-18. Philip had preached the good news to a group of these alienated Jews. They had accepted his words with faith and received Christian baptism. But when Peter and John came from Jerusalem to investigate, they adjudicated that the Spirit 'had not yet fallen on any of them'. Rather than being a theological judgement, that denied the giving of the Holy Spirit in the sacrament of baptism, theirs was an experiential conclusion. When they met the Samaritans, it was immediately apparent that they had not shared in the ecstatic joy and gifts they had received at Pentecost. So the apostles prayed for them 'that they might receive the Holy Spirit'.

While I know that scripture scholars make the valid point that, in this text, Luke is saying that the outpouring of Pentecostal grace in the early church was associated with the apostles, and not evangelists like Philip, scripture scholar Francis Martin once assured me that the first interpretation is also valid. When Peter and John prayed for the Samaritans, the Spirit they had received in a sacramental way in their baptism was released in an active, experiential way, within them. It led them to praise God with joy. Surely it is much the same for many contemporary Catholics. In spite of receiving the sacraments of baptism and confirmation, there is little evidence that the Spirit has fallen on them!

The Irish bishops have described baptism in the Spirit as 'a conversion gift through which one receives a new and significant commitment to the Lordship of Jesus and openness to the power and gifts of the Holy Spirit.' Catholics regard such adult in-fillings of the Spirit as a consequence of the graces already received in the sacraments of baptism and confirmation. As a result, scholars like George Montague and Killian Mc Donnell make the challenging assertion that the in-filling of the Holy Spirit is not only an essential aspect of the sacraments of initiation, it is necessary for all Christians. The American bishops seemed to endorse this view when they encouraged the whole church to seek an experiential in-filling of the Spirit 'as the power of personal and communal transformation with all the graces and charisms needed for the up-building of the church and for our mission in the world.' It is my belief that every bishop, priest and lay person needs to be repeatedly 'filled with the Spirit' (Eph 5:18), if he or she wants to participate fully in the renewal of the church and effective evangelisation.

15 Universal Salvation?

At the end of his parable about Judgement day, Jesus says that God will commend all those who responded to the needy in a compassionate way. Then the righteous will ask, 'Lord, when did we see you hungry and feed you, or thirsty and give you something to drink? When did we see you a stranger and invite you in, or needing clothes and clothe you? When did we see you sick or in prison and go to visit you?' The King will reply, 'I tell you the truth, whatever you did for one of the least of these brothers of mine, you did for me' (Mt 25:34-40). The *New Jerome Biblical Commentary* points out, 'there is currently much debate over whether the phrase brothers and sisters refers only to Christians or to any people in need.'

There are good grounds for thinking that Jesus only regards his baptised disciples as his brothers and sisters. Through the sacrament of baptism people become the adopted sons and daughters of God and, therefore, the brothers and sisters of Christ. The unbaptised are not family members, they are neighbours. This distinction is implied in a number of texts such as: 'let us do good to all people, and especially to those who are of the household of faith' (Gal 6:10). St Peter said: 'Honour all people. Love your brothers and sisters' (1 Pt 2:17).

However, many scholars say that it is highly significant that this parable about the judgement day clearly goes beyond the distinction that is present in many other New Testament texts to insist that if one person meets the needs of another needy person, he or she is ministering to Christ with them and in them. So if you if you give food or drink to a needy, but non-Christian, asylum seeker here in Ireland, you are giving it to Christ. As Cardinal Joseph Ratzinger has observed: 'Nothing suggests that only the faithful, only believers in the gospel of Christ, are meant here, but rather all people in need, without differentiation.' Evidently, Jesus identified himself so much with the poor and needy, irrespective of their beliefs or behaviour, that to love them was to love him with them and in them.

Commenting on another implication of this parable, the

noted scripture scholar Joachim Jeremias asks the important
question: By what criterion will non-Christians be judged. Are
they lost? Jesus replies in effect, 'Non-Christians have met me in
an anonymous way in my brothers and sisters, for the needy are
family to me, the one who shows love to them has shown it to
me, the friend of the poor.' So at the last judgement, rather than
being asked about their beliefs or lack of them, non-Christians
will be asked about the love that they have shown to the afflicted.
They will be granted the grace of a place in the kingdom of heaven
if they have fulfilled the great commandment of love.
Incredulously they will ask, 'But when did we see you hungry
and feed you, thirsty and give you a drink?' And the Lord will
respond, 'As often as you did it to the least of my brothers and
sisters you did it to me.' In other words, the grace of salvation is
available to them on the grounds of their implicit faith in Christ
as expressed in and through their love for the afflicted (cf Gal
5:6). This is a truly important and consoling point. All those who
show love to the afflicted and needy, whether they are Christian
or not, will enter glory on judgement day.

16 Faith in Adversity

The gospels record the way in which Jesus calmed a storm at sea. Matthew's account reads as follows: 'He got into a boat and his disciples followed him. Suddenly a violent storm came up upon the sea, so that the boat was being swamped with waves; but he was asleep. They came and woke him saying, "Lord save us! We are perishing!" He said to them, "Why are you terrified, O you of little faith?" Then he got up, rebuked the winds and the sea, and there was a great calm. The men were amazed and said, "What sort of man is this, whom even the winds and the sea obey?"' (Mt 8:23-27).

Understandably, the disciples panicked during the violent storm. With good reason, they feared that the boat would sink. So they woke Jesus up and implored his help. He performed a miracle in an authoritative way by rebuking the storm. Immediately, the winds died down and calm returned. And then, instead of commending the disciples for relying on him in their hour of need, Jesus admonished them because of their little faith. A question arises. What did he expect of them? It seems to me that, instead of the fearful trust they displayed, he wanted them to be motivated by an expectant trust that could have found expression in either of two ways.

Firstly, in the past Jesus had encouraged the apostles to have mountain-moving faith. For example, following his cursing of the unfruitful fig tree, he said: 'I tell you the truth, if anyone says to this mountain, "Go, throw yourself into the sea," and does not doubt in his heart but believes that what he says will happen, it will be done for him' (11:23). Perhaps Jesus wanted Peter or one of the other apostles to stand up in the boat and to say an authoritative word of command to the storm, in the firm belief that, if there was no hesitation in his heart, it would have been calmed.

Secondly, in Ps 107:23-32 we are told about sailors who were at their wits end during a storm. We are informed that 'They cried out to the Lord in their trouble, and he brought them out of their distress. He stilled the storm to a whisper; the waves of the sea were hushed. They were glad when it grew calm, and he guided them to their desired haven.'

From a psychological point of view, this story has great symbolic value. We all go through predictable and unpredictable crises in our lives. The boat of our personality can be buffeted by all kinds of inner conflicts. Strange feelings begin to well up from the dark recesses of our unconscious minds. We may feel that are going to be swamped by them to such a point that we will suffer some sort of breakdown. It is at times like these, when we seem to be loosing control of our lives that we have to affirm, in faith, that Christ will either end the storm or be with us in the turmoil. Somehow, he will see us through the period of instability, to peace.

I think that Scottish philosopher, John Mc Murray was correct when he said that the maxim of illusory religion runs: 'Fear not; trust in God and he will see that none of the things you fear will happen to you.' The maxim of real religion, on the contrary, is: 'Fear not; the things that you are afraid of are quite likely to happen to you, but they are nothing to be afraid of.' That is preeminently true, when we trust wholeheartedly in Christ.

17 Two Baptisms

There are two main stages in the Christian life, a childish, beginner's stage, and a more mature, adult one. The inspired author of Hebrews wrote: 'You need milk, not solid food! Anyone who lives on milk, being still an infant, is not acquainted with the teaching about righteousness. But solid food is for the mature' (Heb 5:12-14). It seems to me that the two stages, to which these verses refer, were, in a certain qualified sense, implicit in the public ministry of Jesus.

Jesus experienced two baptisms. There was his 'baptism in the Spirit' at the Jordan. It inaugurated his public ministry and empowered him to proclaim and demonstrate the unconditional love of God. This was obvious when Jesus ministered in his native Galilee. He performed numerous healings and miracles, attracted large crowds and seemed to be very successful. However, Jesus also talked about a second baptism, one which would immerse him in suffering. He said: 'I have a baptism with which to be baptised, and what stress I am under until it is completed' (Lk 12:49).

It reached its climax in Holy Week when success gave way to failure, adulation gave way to hostility, and charismatic activity gave way to apparent powerlessness. For example, when he was hanging on the cross the scorners cried out in Mt 27:42: 'He saved others; he cannot save himself. If he is the king of Israel, let him come down from the cross now, and we will believe in him.' But nothing miraculous happened. Instead the ever faithful Jesus felt abandoned by God and man, and in this state he died.

At this point a question arises. Which baptism did most to inaugurate the coming of the kingdom? Obviously both did. But surely the suffering and death of Jesus did more than his healings and miracles to bear testimony to God's love. As St Paul said: 'God proves his love for us in that while we still were sinners Christ died for us … For Jews demand signs and Greeks desire wisdom, but we proclaim Christ crucified, a stumbling block to Jews and foolishness to Gentiles, but to those who are called, both Jews and Greeks, Christ the power of God and the wisdom of God' (Rom 5:8; 1 Cor 1:22-24).

In his *Spiritual Exercises*, St Ignatius describes two stages of Christian growth. In the first, e.g. the period after a religious awakening, the main dynamic at work is that the person is motivated by a self-centred need to receive the mercy, love, consolations and gifts of God. I may say in passing that there is nothing wrong with this kind of desire; it is prompted by the Lord and is a necessary preparation for the second stage of spiritual development. A problem arises when Christians get stuck at this stage and, for one reason or another, fail to move on to the second.

In the second stage, the main dynamic at work is that the person is motivated by a God-centred desire to be united to Jesus. As Paul said, 'I want to know Christ and the power of his resurrection and the sharing of his sufferings' (Phil 3:10). The person no longer focuses on the gifts or consolations of God, but rather on the God of consolation and the gifts. Inwardly, he or she shifts from asking, 'what can God do for me?' to 'what can I do for God?' As Tom Smail, a Protestant spiritual writer, once wisely observed: 'A need-centred Christianity is hampered and hindered because many involved in it have not been converted from need to obedience, from satisfying themselves to being at God's disposal.'

18 Thy Will be Done

If I were asked, what is the most important ethical teaching of the New Testament, I would have no hesitation in pointing the questioner to something St Paul said: 'Live by the Spirit, and you will not gratify the desires of the sinful nature ... if you are led by the Spirit, you are not under law' (Gal 5:16, 18). A number of scripture scholars agree that this verse is a key to Christian morality.

George Montague has pointed out that the Christian life is not a list of do's and don'ts. It is the gift of being moved by the Spirit of God, and the key to life is to allow the Spirit to lead. Paul clearly speaks of an inspired ethic and of inspired action – and it is not reserved for the holy few but is the birth-right of all believers. A crucial point: When confronted with any moral decision, great or small, the Christian's first question should be 'where does the Spirit lead me in this?'

In a long book on Paul's teaching on the Spirit, Gordon Fee says that, although the phrase 'be guided by the Spirit' occurs only here in the Pauline letters, both the argument in which it occurs and the rest of Pauline theology indicate that this is Paul's basic ethical teaching. H. D. Betz, a Protestant like Fee, concurs. He says that the injunction to walk by the Spirit, sums up the apostle's entire ethic, and therefore defines Paul's concept of the Christian life.

If Christians truly desire to discover God's will, they need to do two things. Firstly, St Paul makes it clear that they can only receive divine inspiration if their lives are moulded by the values and beliefs of Jesus. In Rom 12:2 he says: 'Do not conform any longer to the pattern of this world, but be transformed by the renewing of your mind. Then you will be able to test and approve what God's will is, his good, pleasing and perfect will.' Paul would have been familiar with the Greco-Roman practice of making statues by pouring molten metal into moulds so that they would assume their shapes. Analogously, he was saying to the people, 'don't let yourselves be moulded by the values and beliefs of the secular world, such as a preoccupation with the false god's of pleasure, power and popularity.'

Secondly, scripture also makes it clear that, if we want to be guided by the Spirit, we need the gift of wisdom. No wonder the inspired writer testified: 'For this reason, since the day we heard about you, we have not stopped praying for you and asking God to fill you with the knowledge of his will through all spiritual wisdom and understanding' (Col 1:9). These gifts are conferred by the Spirit: 'As for you, the anointing you received from him remains in you, and you do not need anyone to teach you. But his anointing teaches you about all things' (1 Jn 2:27). Presumably, this includes an inkling of what the Lord wants us to do in the here and now. So we need to pray for the spiritual wisdom to know the will of God. As James 1:5 explains: 'If any of you lacks wisdom, he should ask God, who gives generously to all without finding fault, and it will be given to him.'

The Spirit can lead us, as it led Jesus, by prompting loving impulses within us, especially when we are praying. It can also speak to us through our consciences, an inspiring verse of scripture, the suggestion of another person, or an inner inspiration.

19 Did Jesus Become a Catholic?

There are clear indications in the gospels that Jesus felt that his mission was, first and foremost, directed to his fellow Jews. For example, when he was sending out the apostles to preach, he instructed them to do what he himself usually did: 'Do not go among the Gentiles or enter any town of the Samaritans. Go rather to the lost sheep of Israel' (Mt 10:5). On another occasion he said: 'Do not give dogs what is sacred; do not throw your pearls to pigs' (Mt 7:6). In Mark 7:25-29 we are told that Jesus crossed from Jewish into pagan territory. While there, he was approached by a Greek woman. She had been born in Syrian Phoenicia. She begged him to drive a demon out of her daughter. The account of their encounter raises all sorts of questions.

Firstly, why had Jesus left his native Galilee? Perhaps he withdrew because he was a bit disillusioned by a lack of response to his message, or maybe he just needed a rest in an area where he wouldn't be well known. The text does tell us that he entered a house, 'not wanting anybody to know about it' (Mk 7:24). But evidently, his reputation had preceded him. He was better known than he realised and so the concerned mother sought him out to ask for his help.

Secondly, we get a bit of a shock when we hear how Jesus responded to her. In what appears to be an insensitive and even a prejudiced statement, he says: 'First let the children eat all they want,' he told her, 'for it is not right to take the children's bread and toss it to their dogs.' Scripture scholars lessen the initial uneasiness that these words evoke, when they point out that rather than using the word for wild 'dogs', Jesus used a less offensive one which normally referred to household 'puppies'. Even so, it was still a bit disrespectful.

It is really surprising to find that the woman was not put off. She was utterly self-forgetful in her response. Her only concern was her daughter's welfare, and it is clear that she had complete confidence in Jesus' ability to help her. So she replied: 'Yes, Lord, but even the dogs under the table eat the children's crumbs.' In other words: 'Even if you help my girl, like a little puppy, it will not impinge on the prior rights of your own people.'

Jesus was really impressed by the woman's fierce love for her daughter and by her firm trust in his ability to exorcise her. He could see that the grace of his Father was active in her, and that she was manifesting the divine will, indirectly, to him. As he had said on two separate occasions: 'No one can come to me unless the Father who sent me draws him or her' (Jn 6:44), and 'I do nothing on my own ... The Son can only do what he sees the Father doing' (Jn 8:28; 5:19). It would seem, therefore, that he saw the Syro-Phoenician woman's loving desire and her firm faith as an indirect revelation of the Father's will for him. He was being led to minister to this Gentile's daughter. So he told her, 'For such a reply, you may go; the demon has left your daughter.'

A question. Did Jesus move, at that moment, from a restricted to a more universal, catholic understanding of his mission? Perhaps he did. This impressive Greek woman represented the Gentile world which would be evangelised, sometime later, by St Paul and his successors.

20 The Look of Love

In New Testament times there were large numbers of disabled and handicapped people. They had to fend for themselves because there was no health care or social welfare. Most people were just about scraping a living, but those who were destitute depended upon their generosity to survive. As you can imagine, beggars were everywhere. They were a noisy, demanding, public nuisance. The cripple at the gate called beautiful was no exception. People were used to the sight of him. He was always in the same place, rattling his begging bowl. Then the apostles Peter and John happened to pass by. He asked them for money in his usual pathetic way. We are told, 'Peter looked straight at him, as did John. Then Peter said, "Look at us!"' (Acts 3:4).

The emphasis on looking is very striking. The apostles had a special way of looking at the man and they wanted him to reciprocate by looking at them in a new way. Maybe it is fanciful, but I imagine that the look of the apostles was contemplative. The word in English comes from the Latin, *contemplari*, meaning 'to look at, to pay sustained attention'. I also imagine that their look was respectful and reverential. The word 'respect' in English comes from the Latin, *respicere*, which means 'to look again'. In other words, the apostles did not judge the beggar by human appearances. They looked beyond his handicap, rags and off-putting manner to see and reverence the sacred presence of Christ, who is present in the least of his brethren.

Peter and John were well aware that the beggar had got used to seeing people in utilitarian terms, as potential almsgivers. They wanted him to switch his attention from the alms he hoped to get from the givers, to the givers of the alms. We are told: 'So the man gave them his attention, expecting to get something from them' (Acts 3:5). While he does pay attention to the two men, he is still focusing in a rather self-centred, impersonal way on the money he is hoping for. While his reaction is understandable, it is regrettable because it is so impersonal. Clearly, his poverty has dehumanised him to a certain extent. He is crippled emotionally and spiritually, as well as physically.

By looking at the crippled man with reverence, the apostles were witnessing to the unconditional and affirming love of Christ. Like his Master, Peter demonstrated the liberating reality of that love by saying, 'Silver or gold I do not have, but what I have I give you. In the name of Jesus Christ of Nazareth, walk' (Acts 3:6). We are informed that 'instantly the man's feet and ankles became strong. He jumped to his feet and began to walk' (3:8). Surely, the cripple's outward healing was matched by an inner healing that affirmed his dignity and restored his self-esteem as a person who was truly loved by God. As a result he would have looked at himself, the apostles, and the Lord in a new way.

One implication of this story is that Christians have to develop a more contemplative and reverential way of paying attention to people, especially the poor. I have found that what they crave, more than anything else, is the alms of understanding love. It is best expressed in the form of a listening ear and an empathic heart. Just as a sculptor can look beyond the rough surface of a block of stone to see a lovely figure locked within, so too we have to see what the divine Artist sees, and enable it to be set free.

21 God is a Verb

In one of his writings, Von Goethe described how Dr Faustus wanted to translate the bible into German. He said: 'Our spirits yearn toward revelation. That nowhere glows more fair, more excellent, than here in the New Testament.' Later on, the doctor wrestled with the translation of John 1:1. He said: 'It is written: "In the beginning was the word!" Dissatisfied with that rendition, he went on to write "In the beginning was the thought." He followed that version with, "In the beginning was the power!" Finally, he concluded, "The Spirit's helping me! I see now what I need and write assured: In the beginning was the Deed!"' Two hundred years later, the American designer, Buckminster Fuller encapsulated Von Goethe's point when he said: 'to me God is a verb, not a noun.' This dynamic notion of God is attractive and relevant in our fast changing society, permeated, as it is, by the notion of evolution. It is also very biblical.

Unlike modern philosophers, who argue for and against the existence of God, the bible takes it for granted. Psalm 53:1 says in typical fashion: 'Only the fool says in his heart, "There is no God."' For their part, the scriptures focus on the saving activity of God in history. Let's focus on one outstanding example. In the Lord's Prayer we say: 'Hallowed be thy name.' For many years I thought that this petition was primarily calling on believers to praise and worship the holy name of God. While there is some truth in this interpretation, it is not the main one.

Rather than focusing on what we can do to bring honour to God, this petition primarily calls on God to demonstrate the holiness of the divine name by means of saving and liberating deeds performed among us. They help to establish God's reign of justice and peace in the world. The background of this interpretation is to be found in Ezech 36:21-23 which reads: 'I had concern for my holy name, which the house of Israel profaned among the nations where they had gone ... I will show the holiness of my great name, which has been profaned, among the nations, the name you have profaned among them. Then the nations will know that I am the Lord, declares the Sovereign

Lord, when I show myself holy through you before their eyes.'
God demonstrates the holiness of the divine name by means of
liberating deeds.

There is evidence that Jesus espoused this dynamic notion of
God. For example, on one occasion he said: 'My Father is always
at his work to this very day, and I, too, am working.' (Jn 5:17).
When we look at the life and ministry of Jesus we see how he
laboured ceaselessly on people's behalf. For example, when
John the Baptist was in prison, he sent messengers to ask Jesus if
he was the promised Messiah. Instead of giving any kind of
theoretical answer, 'Jesus replied, "Go back and report to John
what you hear and see: The blind receive sight, the lame walk,
those who have leprosy are cured, the deaf hear, the dead are
raised, and the good news is preached to the poor"' (Mt 11:4-5).

It would also be true to say that the words 'hallowed be thy
name' have their eye on the second coming when the holiness of
God's name will be vindicated, in a definitive way. In the meantime, we believers need to co-operate with God's purposes by
working to usher in the kingdom. As Psalm 37:5 says: 'Commit
your way to the Lord, trust in him and he will act.'

22 Asylum Seekers

In the Old Testament the Jewish people were very clannish. The word neighbour was restricted to fellow Israelites. It did not extend to foreigners. Jews were to love their neighbours, but they didn't have to love anyone who was not a neighbour, such as foreign gentiles or enemies. However, when they themselves were captives in Egypt, they learned from first hand personal experience what it was like to be a despised and alien group in a foreign land. When their captivity finally ended they moved to the promised land. Over the years many foreigners came to live among them. These people didn't belong to either the Jewish race or to its religion. Strictly speaking they were not neighbours. Nevertheless, the scriptures indicated that the Lord cared for them. As Psalm 146:9 says: 'The Lord watches over the alien and sustains the fatherless and the widow.'

A number of Old Testament texts said that the Jewish people should treat the foreigners in their midst as if they were neighbours. For example in Lev 19:33-34 Yahweh said: 'When an alien lives with you in your land, do not mistreat him. The alien living with you must be treated as one of your native-born. Love him as yourself, for you were aliens in Egypt. I am the Lord your God.' Again, in Lev 25:35, the Lord said: 'If one of your countrymen becomes poor and is unable to support himself among you, help him as you would an alien or a temporary resident, so he can continue to live among you.' Speaking about the judicial system which could be biased against immigrants, God stated: 'I charged your judges at that time: Hear the disputes between your brothers and judge fairly, whether the case is between brother Israelites or between one of them and an alien' (Deut 1:16).

It would seem to me that Jesus built upon the best of Old Testament thinking about the distinction between neighbours and aliens, when he extended the notion of neighbour to include anyone and everyone. That is the main point in the parable of the Good Samaritan. Having told the story about the unfortunate man who had been mugged and robbed, Jesus described

how three of his fellow Jews ignored his plight while a
Samaritan, an alien, went to great efforts to help him. Jesus
asked: 'Which of these three do you think was a neighbour to the
man who fell into the hands of robbers?' The expert in the law
replied, 'The one who had mercy on him.' Jesus told him, 'Go
and do likewise' (Lk 10:36-37).

Surely, these biblical teachings are relevant in contemporary
Ireland. Like the Jews who lived in Egypt, many of our people
have had to live as foreigners in countries such as Britain,
America and Australia. But now things are changing. Happily,
like the Jews of old, many of our emigrants are returning home.
But besides these native Irish men and women, tens of thousands of economic migrants and asylum seekers are coming
from all over the world to live and work in Ireland. It results in
many problems of assimilation due to differences in race, culture, language, and religion. Consequently, the foreigners amongst
us can be treated with mistrust, suspicion, prejudice and even
hatred. As a Christian country, we Irish are faced with the religious challenge of treating the strangers amongst us as neighbours, deserving of our respect and love. But as St James warns
us: 'If you show favouritism, you commit sin and are convicted
by the law as transgressors' (Jas 2:9).

23 Sport and Spirituality

In ancient Greece, the Isthmian Games were second only to the Olympics in order of importance. They were held in the late spring of every second year, in a stadium that was about six miles from Corinth. We know that they were held in 51 AD around the time when Paul was living in the locality. It is quite possible that he made tents for sale during the games, and attended some of them when he had the time. So it is not surprising that he used a sporting analogy in order to make a spiritual point. He said: 'Do you not know that in a race all the runners run, but only one gets the prize? Run in such a way as to get the prize. Everyone who competes in the games goes into strict training. They do it to get a crown that will not last; but we do it to get a crown that will last forever. Therefore I do not run like a man running aimlessly; I do not fight like a man beating the air. No, I beat my body and make it my slave so that after I have preached to others, I myself will not be disqualified for the prize' (1 Cor 9:24-27).

Paul highlights two sports. Firstly, there was the footrace. Those involved had to prepare well. They had to swear, by Zeus, to follow ten months of strict training beforehand. Secondly, boxing was another of the major competitions at Greek games. A boxer had to discipline his body by working out with tough sparring partners if he was to have any hope of winning. Paul says that, just as these athletes had to train in a disciplined, single-minded way, to win a perishable crown of dry celery, so Christians need to engage in rigorous spiritual exercises in order to win the imperishable crown of eternal life.

In modern Christianity, spiritual exercises are sometimes referred to as ascetical practices. The words 'ascetic' and 'asceticism' are derived from the Greek *asketes*, which refers to a person in training, and *askeein* 'to exercise.' Christians realise that just as working-out is vital for success in modern sports, especially professional ones, so it is equally vital in spirituality. Good intentions are not enough. Self-indulgent tendencies need to be overcome if people are to carry out the great command of loving

others in the way that Jesus has loved us. As Paul perceptively
observes: 'When I want to do good, evil is right there with me.
For in my inner being I delight in God's law; but I see another
law at work in the members of my body, waging war against the
law of my mind and making me a prisoner of the law of sin at
work within my members' (Rom 7:21-23). So conscientious
Christians deny themselves legitimate pleasures, especially during
Lent. They do so by means of such things as fasting, voluntary
work, prayer, spiritual reading and almsgiving. They engage in
these practices in order to bring the selfish urgings of their bodies into obedience to their higher spiritual aspirations, values
and beliefs.

Hopefully, as a result of spiritual exercises like these they
will be able to say at life's end: 'I have fought the good fight, I
have finished the race, I have kept the faith. Now there is in store
for me the crown of righteousness, which the Lord, the righteous Judge, will award to me on that day – and not only to me,
but also to all who have longed for his appearing' (2 Tim 4:7-8).

24 Temptation

When a person experiences a spiritual awakening, he or she often endures a time of testing. They have a heightened sense of good and evil. This was the way with Jesus. Filled with the Spirit he underwent a time of temptation as described in Lk 4:2-13. The devil urged him to abandon his God-given vocation as suffering servant in order to become the political messiah of popular expectation.

Should one see the devil, in this gospel account, as a fallen angel, or as a mythical figure who personifies the dark side of the unconscious mind? Pope Paul VI stated the church's belief when he wrote: 'It is a departure from the picture provided by biblical and church teaching to refuse to acknowledge the devil's existence; to regard him as a self-sustaining principle, who, unlike other creatures, does not owe his origin to God; or to explain the devil as a pseudo-reality, a conceptual and fanciful personification of the unknown causes of our misfortunes.' So Jesus was really and truly tempted by the evil one.

When Jesus was invited to turn stones to bread, it represented an urge to imitate Moses who had promised the people that they would be fed by manna from the heavens. He could do this by devoting himself to the alleviation of hunger and poverty. While this might be a laudible thing to do, whether by social action or miraculously, it would not be best. He recalled the words of Deut 8:3, 'Man does not live by bread alone, but by every word that comes from the mouth of God.'

The devil offered Jesus the kingdoms of the world if only he would worship him. At that time Caesar ruled the known world. If Jesus was willing to lead the Zealots, whose political ambitions were motivated by religious ideals, he could conquer the Roman empire for God. He would do this by means of armed struggle. But Jesus realised that this would be alien to God's will for him and so he quoted Deut 6:13: 'Fear the Lord your God and serve him only.'

Finally, the devil tempted Jesus to act in an irresponsible way by jumping from the Royal Porch of the temple in Jerusalem into the Kidron valley, 450 feet below. If he did this, he could rely on God to bear him up in a miraculous way. This wondrous, charismatic event would lead to mass conversions. Again Jesus resisted, this time, by quoting Deut 6:16: 'Do not put the Lord your God to the test.'

It is significant that Jesus resisted each of the devil's temptations with inspired scripture texts which are, as Paul tells us, the sword of the Spirit (Eph 6:17). They warded off the evil one for the time being. Ominously, he would return in the future, especially during passion week.

When he spoke to the Irish people in Limerick on 1 October 1979, Pope John Paul II uttered these prophet words: 'Your country seems in a sense to be living again the temptations of Christ: Ireland is being asked to prefer the kingdoms of this world and their splendour to the kingdom of God. Satan the tempter, the adversary of Christ, will use all his might and all his deceptions to win Ireland for the way of the world ... Now is the time of testing for Ireland. This generation is once more a generation of decision. Dear sons and daughters of Ireland, pray ... Pray that Ireland may not fail in the test. Pray as Jesus taught us to pray: Lead us not into temptation but deliver us from evil.'

25 Was Jesus Emotional?

A careful reading of the gospels indicates that Jesus was an emotional man. The Son of God was deeply affected by everything he experienced. He did not edit or censor his impressions by means of unconscious defence mechanisms. As a result, he displayed an almost childlike openness and emotional vulnerability. His was the perception of an Adam or Eve before the fall, wholehearted and innocent. Let's look at representative examples of his emotions such as anger, frustration, sorrow, anguish, joy, love and compassion.

Many pious portraits of Jesus depict him as an inoffensive man, meek and mild, who would never have been selected to play on a rugby team. In reality he was nothing of the kind. He was a strong, passionate person, who was preoccupied with the honour of God. He experienced righteous anger and wasn't afraid to express it when he cursed a fig tree that had failed to bear fruit (Mk 11:14) and threw the money changers out of the temple (Jn 2:15). Why these strong reactions? 'His disciples remembered that it was written, "Zeal for Your house has eaten me up"' (Jn 2:17).

Jesus got frustrated because of people's lack of insight and faith. Remember the time the apostles failed to exorcise an epileptic boy. When his father brought him to Jesus he said in an exasperated way: 'O unbelieving generation, how long shall I stay with you? How long shall I put up with you?' (Mk 9:19). On another occasion Jesus was disillusioned when Philip said: 'Show us the Father.' He answered with apparent sadness and frustration: 'Don't you know me, Philip, even after I have been among you such a long time? Anyone who has seen me has seen the Father. How can you say, "Show us the Father"?' (Jn 14:9).

Jesus was also capable feeling fear and anguish. Speaking of such emotions the author of Heb 5:7 says: 'He offered up prayers and petitions with loud cries and tears to the one who could save him from death.' We are told on another occasion: 'As Jesus approached Jerusalem and saw the city, he wept over it' (Lk 19:41). This was because he had a premonition that it would be destroyed in the future. He also wept and groaned with sorrow at the funeral of Lazarus (Jn 11:35). Later on the cross he felt abandoned and cried out: 'My God, my God, why have you forsaken me?' (Mk 15:34).

Jesus often experienced positive emotions. For example, he rejoiced because God had revealed the mysteries of the kingdom to the poor. The text implies that he was so ecstatically happy that he leapt for joy (Mt 11:25). He was astonished by the centurion's faith (Mt 8:10). On another occasion, when a young man informed the Lord he had kept the commandments from his youth: 'Jesus looked at him and loved him' (Mk 10:20-21). Still other texts inform us that the words and deeds of Jesus were motivated by a strong sense of empathy for the afflicted. For example, when needy people followed him into the wilderness, 'he had compassion on them, because they were harassed and helpless, like sheep without a shepherd' (Mt 9:36). The Greek of the gospel implies that he was moved to the pit of his stomach by the people's troubles.

If we want to be human, like Jesus, we need to be people of feeling, unafraid of spontaneous emotional responses. Remember, the Lord has promised: 'I will give you a new heart and put a new spirit in you; I will remove from you your heart of stone and give you a heart of flesh' (Ezek 36:26).

26 Saving Faith

The author of Heb 11:6 tells us that, 'without faith it is impossible to please God.' He had saving, or justifying faith particularly in mind. Catholics tend to talk about the former and Protestants about the latter, but in reality both are biblical. In November 1999, a joint declaration on the doctrine of justification was published by the Roman Catholic Church and the Lutheran World Federation. Paragraph 15 contained these momentous words: 'Together we confess by grace alone, in faith in Christ's saving work and not because of any merit on our part, we are accepted by God and receive the Holy Spirit, who renews our hearts while equipping and calling us to good works.' This statement heals the main rift that occurred so acrimoniously at the time of the Reformation. Not only that, it has its roots planted firmly in the scriptures.

The notion of justification, of being put at rights with God, was implicit in Jesus' parable about the prodigal son. He was accepted back into the family home, not because of any personal merit or good works, but because he accepted that his Father's love was unconditional. It seems to me that saving faith involves at least four interconnected elements.

Firstly, there is an acknowledgment of a need for salvation. Anyone with an ounce of sense would acknowledge that we all fall short of what God, through our consciences, expects of us. As one of the psalms says: 'If you O Lord should mark our guilt, Lord who would survive?' (130:3). The answer to this rhetorical question is, no one! This awareness was evident when the despairing Roman jailer cried out to Paul and Silas, 'What must I do to be saved?' in Acts 16:30.

Secondly, the needy person has to hear about the forgiveness that is available to those who trust in Christ. As Paul said: 'Faith comes from what is heard, and what is heard comes through the word of Christ' (Rom 10:17). It is as if God were saying through the members of the church: 'Believe in the Lord Jesus, and you will be saved, you and your household' (Acts 16:31). In other words: 'Don't worry about God's justice. Though real, it is on hold until the judgement day. The good news is this. You are living in the glorious era of God's unrestricted mercy and love. If you look into the eyes of God's merciful love, expecting only merciful love, you will receive only merciful love, now and at the hour of your death.'

Thirdly, as Acts 16:31 points out, it is by believing in the Lord Jesus Christ, rather than trusting in our own efforts or merits, that we are saved. Paul declared, 'We have come to believe in Christ Jesus, so that we might be justified by faith in Christ, and not by doing the works of the law' (Gal 2:16). When this grace is given to us, the truth falls from head to heart in a liberating way. We realise that, as a result of trusting completely in the good news, there is no condemnation in Christ. We are declared not guilty and acquitted by the grace of God.

Fourthly, belief leads to confession. Paul expressed it this way: 'If you confess with your mouth that Jesus is Lord and believe in your heart that God raised him from the dead, you will be saved. For one believes with the heart and so is justified, and one confesses with the mouth and so is saved' (Rom 10:9-10). We can bear witness to our salvation by means of thanksgiving prayer, living in a Christian way and sharing our story with others.

27 God's Love

God the Father loved Jesus with a perfect, and everlasting love. It was no more than he deserved. As the divine Son of God, he was endowed with every perfection of divinity. As Jesus testified: 'The Father loves the Son' (Jn 3:35). What is quite amazing, and quite incomprehensible, is the fact that Jesus loves us in the same way, as if we, like him, were divine. As he said: 'As the Father loves me, so I love you' (Jn 17:23).

Jesus showed his love for each one of us in many different ways. He said: 'The greatest love a person can have for friends is to give his life for them. And you are my friends' (Jn 15:13). St Paul added sometime later: 'You see, at just the right time, when we were still powerless, Christ died for the ungodly. Very rarely will anyone die for a righteous man, though for a good man someone might possibly dare to die. But God demonstrates his own love for us in this: While we were still sinners, Christ died for us' (Rom 5:6-8).

From the time of his conversion onwards, Paul enjoyed a vivid personal experience of that love. 'This life I live now,' he said, 'I live by faith in the Son of God who loved me and gave his life for me' (Gal 2:20). St Paul knew that we can only come to know the unmerited love of Jesus through an outpouring of the Holy Spirit. As he says: 'God has poured out his love into our hearts by the Holy Spirit, whom he has given us' (Rom 5:5). As a result, he asks, in one of his most beautiful prayers, 'that you, being rooted and established in love, may have power, together with all the saints, to grasp how wide and long and high and deep is the love of Christ, and to know this love that surpasses knowledge – that you may be filled to the measure of all the full-ness of God' (Eph 3:17-19).

This prayer can be answered, either in a gradual way as a re-sult of a number of incremental touches of divine grace, or by means of a sudden spiritual awakening, such as that enjoyed by St Thérèse of Lisieux. It occurred on her night of 'illumination', during midnight Mass, Christmas 1886. She says: 'Charity found its way into my heart and I knew what God wanted of me.'

Whether they occur gradually or suddenly, adult conversion experiences lead to an awareness where 'We ourselves know and
believe the love which God has for us' (1 Jn 4:19).

How should we respond to the gift of such an amazing love?
'As I have loved you,' said Jesus, 'so you must love one another.
By this all men will know that you are my disciples, if you love
one another' (Jn 13:34-35). Later, Paul went on to describe the
qualities of that love. It is: 'patient, and kind. It does not envy, it
does not boast, it is not proud. It is not rude, it is not self-seeking,
it is not easily angered, it keeps no record of wrongs. Love does
not delight in evil but rejoices with the truth. It always protects,
always trusts, always hopes, always perseveres' (1 Cor 13:4-7).
When the word love, in this quotation, is replaced with the name
of Jesus, one has a mini portrait of the Son of God!

We need to repeatedly savour these life-giving truths in a
prayerful way because the Christian life needs to be built on the
foundation stone of a personal experience of God's love.

28 Faith and Good Works

At the end of the 90s an important booklet was published. It was called: *Evangelicals and Catholics Together in Ireland*. Significantly, it included a joint statement on the subject of justification, i.e. right relationship with God. Among other things it said: 'We agree that justification is not earned by any good works or merits of our own: it is entirely God's gift, conferred through the Father's sheer graciousness, out of the love he bears us in his Son, who suffered on our behalf and rose from the dead for our justification. Jesus was "put to death for our trespasses and raised for our justification" (Rom 4:25).' This assertion draws attention to a foundational Christian truth which is clearly illustrated by the story of the Prodigal Son (Lk 15:11-32).

The typically merit-based attitude of the elder brother was described by Rabbi Jehuda:

If you behave like children
You are called children.
If you do not behave like children
You are not called children.

Rabbi Meir described the grace-filled attitude of the Father when he added, 'Either way, you are called children.' In other words, your status as beloved children of God depends on the Father's love, not on personal merit.

You will recall how the younger brother claimed his inheritance, which was tantamount to wishing his father was dead, and headed off to do his own thing in a foreign land where Jewish laws did not apply. When things turned sour for him he came to his senses and decided to go home: 'I will set out and go back to my father and say to him: Father, I have sinned against heaven and against you. I am no longer worthy to be called your son; make me like one of your hired men' (Lk 15:18-19). As we know, the Father spotted him in the distance. He ran to greet him. When his son tried to make his pathetic confession, the Father brushed his words aside and embraced him. For his part, the son needed the humility to accept that his father's compassionate love couldn't be forfeited by his bad behaviour. It was a free, unmerited gift of the parent who loved him unconditionally.

When the elder brother heard about the wonderful reception his younger sibling had received, he was resentful. He felt that that his Father's love for the black sheep of the family was unfair. After all, he had remained at home and worked hard on the farm. Surely, he had earned his father's affection and gifts. 'My son,' the father said, 'you are always with me, and everything I have is yours' (Lk 15:31). In other words, 'you could have taken the cloak of honour, the ring of authority, the shoes of freedom and killed the fatted calf, at any time you liked. My love for you is unconditional. You could no more earn it by your good behaviour than your brother could forfeit it by his bad behaviour. For my part, I hope you continue to work hard on the farm as a grateful response to my unconditional love, which you already have, rather than as a means of trying to earn that love, as heretofore.'

Surely, there is a bit of the elder and younger brother in each of us. Either way, we should come to God with empty hands, neither trusting in our good works, or worrying about the lack of them. We trust, solely, in the unconditional mercy and love of Christ. It will put us in right relationship with God. Then, lovingly we express our thanks in good works.

29 The Golden Rule

In the Old Testament there was an important ethical guideline, which is sometimes referred to as the silver rule. It says: 'Do to no one what you would not done to you' (Job 4:15). It is a guideline that is found in this negative form in the writings of two great Jewish scholars, Hillel and Philo of Alexandria, and in the *Analects* of Confucius. It also appears in one form or another in the writings of Plato, Aristotle, Isocrates, and Seneca. It was reiterated in the *Didache*, one of the earliest Christian documents: 'The Way of Life is this: You shall ... do nothing to any person that you would not wish to be done to yourself.'

In the gospels, Jesus gave this ethical precept a more positive spin when he advocated the 'golden rule'. One version states: 'Do to others as you would have them do to you' (Lk 6:31). The other says: 'In everything do to others what you would have them do to you, for this sums up the Law and the Prophets' (Mt 7:12). Commenting on these verses, William Barclay's observes: 'This is probably the most universally famous thing that Jesus ever said. With this commandment the Sermon on the Mount reaches its summit. This saying of Jesus has been called the capstone of the whole discourse. It is the topmost peak of social ethics, and the Everest of all ethical teaching.'

This teaching takes on new meaning when we recall that Jesus practiced this rule in his own life. He wanted what was best for people. He had a deep insight into their innermost needs, sometimes because people told him about them, and on other occasions because he had an intuitive or inspired awareness of what was best for them. Then, metaphorically, Jesus wrapped a towel around his waist and humbly served people in accordance with their needs. Surely, this insight Christianises the Golden Rule. It is as if Jesus is saying, 'You know from experience how I express my love to you. Now love one another; even as I have loved you, that is, by observing the Golden Rule.'

To love in this Christian way, two things are needed – goodwill and insight. A person with goodwill wants what's best for another. But that is not enough. Benevolence needs to be accompanied by an accurate awareness of the needs of the other person, which may be quite different from one's own. For instance if a grandfather gave a granddaughter a present of a hearing aid or walking stick he himself would like to receive, it would, clearly, be absurd. But because they love another person, and wish one another well, loving people, quite often, wrongly presume that they know what is best for the other person.

Insight is the fruit of empathy. It is the ability to take off one's own mental and emotional shoes, in order to stand in those of the other person. Empathy can be defined as the ability to enter into and understand the inner world of another person and to communicate that understanding to him or her. Then the loving person responds accordingly, either in the form of sensitive emotional support, or appropriate practical action. I suspect that this is what St Paul had in mind when he wrote: 'Do nothing out of selfish ambition or vain conceit, but in humility consider others better than yourselves. Each of you should look not only to your own interests, but also to the interests of others' (Phil 2:3-4). He said something similar in Rom 12:10: 'Be devoted to one another in brotherly love. Honour one another above yourselves.'

30 The Scriptures are Inspired

In the bible, the Hebrew and Greek words for spirit literally meant, 'breath' because breath and life were considered to be synonymous. While a person was still breathing, the spirit was still in the body. With this in mind we can look at an important scriptural assertion. In 2 Tim 3:16 we read: 'All scripture is God-breathed,' in other words, all scripture is inspired by the Holy Spirit. There is a related text in 2 Pet 1:20-21 which states: 'You must understand that no prophecy of scripture came about by the prophet's own interpretation. For prophecy never had its origin in the will of man, but men spoke from God as they were carried along by the Holy Spirit.'

Commenting on this notion of inspiration the *Catechism of the Catholic Church* says, in pars 105-107, that the church accepts that the Old and New Testaments were 'written under the inspiration of the Holy Spirit. They have God as their author. They have been handed on as such to the church herself. To compose the sacred books, God chose certain men who, all the while he employed them in this task, made full use of their own faculties and powers so that, though he acted in them and by them, it was as true authors that they consigned to writing whatever he wanted written, and no more. The inspired books teach the truth.' This latter statement echoes the teaching of par 11 of Vatican II's, *Constitution on the Word of God*. 'The Books of scripture must be acknowledged as teaching firmly, faithfully, and without error that truth which God wanted put into the sacred writings for the sake of our salvation.'

Do Catholics believe that everything the bible says, whether poetic, mythical, historical, scientific, or religious, is completely true? Yes and no. We now know that the book of Jonah is, in all likelihood, not historically accurate. It's description of the unfortunate prophet being swallowed by a whale is an inspired parable, which seeks to illustrate religious truths about God's desire to convert all nations to accept Yahweh, and to lead a moral life. The same thing could be said of the Book of Genesis. Instead of teaching scientific facts about the dynamics of creation, the first

book of the bible teaches theological truths, such as the belief
that all created things ultimately depend upon God for their on-
going existence.

When one reads the gospels, it becomes evident that they are
contradictory on a number of factual points. For instance,
Matthew says that at the time of Jesus' birth, Mary and Joseph
lived in Bethlehem. Sometime later, after their sojourn in Egypt,
they returned to live in Nazareth. The text implies that they had
never lived there before. In Luke's account of the nativity, Mary
and Joseph were living in Nazareth and went to Bethlehem for
the census, where Jesus was born. They returned soon afterwards to Nazareth without any mention of an intervening visit
to Egypt. A non-fundamentalist notion of inspiration and in-
errency maintains that while the theological truths connected
with the birth of Jesus are inspired and true, not all the attendant
historical details are necessarily accurate. Some of them may
have been borrowed from 1 Sam 2:1-26.

So, while it is true that Catholics believe in the inspiration of
the scriptures, we do so in a nuanced, non-literal way. With the
help of biblical scholarship, the wheat of theological truth has to
be separated from the chaff of circumstantial facts, whether scientific or historical. In this way the modern day Christian can
feed on the nourishing bread of biblical truth.

31 Jesus and Sepphoris

Some time ago I came across a fascinating fact that threw new light on the life of Jesus. As you know, our Lord was from Galilee which had a population of 200,000. He grew up in Nazareth which housed about 34 families and had a population of about 400. It had cisterns for water, olive presses, vats for oil, together with silos and millstones for grain. It is clear that the principal occupation was agriculture. There was no evidence of wealth.

Three and a half miles from Nazareth was the Greco-Roman city of Sepphoris. It was built on a hill 400 feet in height, and had a population of about 30-40,000 people, most of whom were Jewish. Scripture scholars maintain that when Jesus said to the disciples: 'You are ... a city set on a hill which cannot be hidden' (Mt 5:14), he might well have had Sepphoris in mind. Archaeology has discovered that, in spite of the Roman occupation and Greek influences, the city was very Jewish. There is little evidence of the usual foreign characteristics, such as a gymnasium, chariot racing course, roofed theatre, decorated fountain, pagan shrine or sanctuary.

Apparently, the Romans had destroyed Sepphhoris when Jesus was about two. It was being rebuilt, fortified and beautified by Herod Antipas during Jesus' lifetime. It included a luxurious royal palace, bank, administrative offices, archives, water system, fortress and a 4,500 seat amphitheatre. There were two main streets, paved with diamond-shaped slabs of stone and bordered by two colonnades. With good reason it was referred to as the jewel of Galilee. If Jesus climbed a ridge near Nazareth he would have been able to see Sepphoris in the distance. There is a traditional belief that Jesus' grandparents, Joachim and Anna, lived there, and that his mother Mary was born in the city. He could have walked to it in less than an hour. Presumably he visited it on numerous occasions.

Although it is never mentioned in the gospels, Sepphoris must have exercised some influence on Jesus. For instance, the scriptures tell us that Joseph was a 'carpenter' (Mt 5:14; Mk 6:3).

Scholars point out that the Greek word *tekton*, which is used by the evangelists, can also be translated as 'artisan, stone mason, builder, or craftsman'. So it has been suggested that it is quite possible that Joseph and Jesus were involved in construction work in the city. If that were the case, Jesus would probably have learned to speak some Greek.

Scholars have also suggested that Jesus' many references to kings may have been based on his experience of Herod Antipas. On one occasion he warned the people to avoid 'the leaven of Herod' (Mk 8:15). Jesus also spoke on seventeen occasions about hypocrites and hypocrisy. For example, he said: 'When you fast, do not look sombre as the hypocrites do' (Mt 6:16). The words may have been derived from the world of theatre, because the Greek word *hypokrites* can be translated as 'actor, or pretender'. Jesus thought that many of the people of the time, especially the scribes and Pharisees, honoured God with their lips but not with their hearts (Mk 7:1-8). However, another scholar, called Barr, has pointed out that hypocrites can also mean 'self-righteousness' and, therefore, wouldn't have any connection with the theatrical world.

The traditional image of Jesus as a rough and ready, rural peasant, with little or no idea of urban living, is quite obviously mistaken. Even if he didn't work in Sepphoris, rarely visited the city, and never attended its theatre, he must have had first hand knowledge of its ethos as a multi-cultural city.

32 He Descended into Hell

Many years ago a priest said to me, 'I don't think the Apostles Creed should contain the phrase 'he descended into hell'. It is meaningless and irrelevant.' I suppose he had a point. While the phrase is included in the Athanasian Creed, it is omitted from the Nicene Creed which we recite at Mass every Sunday. In this reflection I want to highlight the scriptural meaning of this phrase, while indicating why it has spiritual relevance today.

The Jews of the Old Testament believed that after death people went to *sheol*, in Hebrew, or *Hades*, in Greek. It was the realm of the living dead. It was thought of as a subterranean region clothed in thick darkness, from which it was impossible to return. In the New Testament, Jesus spoke of hell as *Gehenna*, the place where lost souls suffered punishment (Mt 5:29-30; 10:28). The word was derived from a rubbish dump outside Jerusalem. It was always burning and was associated with a loathsome type of worm.

When the creed tells us that Jesus descended into hell, it means that he descended into *sheol* rather than *Gehenna*. This phrase can be understood in two interrelated ways. Firstly, when Jesus cried out on the cross: 'My God, my God, why have you forsaken me?' (Mt 27:46), he had already begun to enter *sheol* from a psychological and spiritual point of view. Nailed to the cross he was suspended between heaven and earth, shrouded in darkness, and separated from people and God.

When Jesus commended his soul to God, his physical death radicalised his limbo experience. He entered the valley of the dry bones mentioned in Ezech 37:4. Scripture tells us that: 'in the spirit he visited the spirits in prison (*sheol*), and preached to them ... so that although their bodies were punished with death, they could still live in their spirits as God lives' (1 Pet 3:18-20; 4:6). Jesus' descent into *sheol*, to be with the spirits of the dead, was his ultimate act of abnegation and solidarity. Not only did he share in their alienation, he also shared the good news about God's free offer of unconditional mercy and love. They were evangelised by this prophetic message. As a result, they were released from their imprisonment. In Mt 27:52-53 we are told in mythical language: 'The tombs broke open and the bodies of many holy people who had died were raised to life. They came out of the tombs, and after Jesus' resurrection they went into the holy city and appeared to many people' (cf Acts 2:24; Eph 4:8-10).

We all go through hellish experiences. Typically, we feel at breaking point, in the dark emotionally and spiritually, and disconnected from people and from God. We might identify with some or all of these words of French atheist, Jean Paul Sartre: 'I sent Heaven messages: no reply. Heaven doesn't even know my name. I kept wondering what I was in God's eyes. Now I know the answer: nothing. God doesn't see me, God doesn't hear me, God doesn't know me. You see the void above our heads? That is God. You see the hole in the ground? That's what God is. You see the crack in the door? That's God too. Silence is God. Absence is God. God is human loneliness.' At moments like these, it is comforting to realise that Jesus has entered into, and shared, our state of isolation and distress. But then, at God's appointed time, desolation of spirit will turn to consolation. Our hearts will once again burn within us as we experience his liberating and life-giving Holy Spirit.

33 Forgiveness

I'm utterly confident that God offers every one of us unconditional mercy. This, wonderful gift is available to all of us, all of
the time. However, we can only receive and appropriate that
saving grace when we are willing to offer the same mercy – with
no strings attached – to those who have hurt or injured us in any
way. I say this because it is the clear, consistent and unambigu-
ous teaching of the scriptures. Let us look at the evidence.

Sir 28:2-4 says: 'Pardon your neighbour any wrongs done to
you, and when you pray, your sins will be forgiven. If anyone
nurses anger against another, can one then demand compassion
from the Lord? Showing no pity for someone like oneself, can
one then plead for one's own sins?' The principle of reciprocity
is evident in this verse. However, it would probably be true to
say that the notion of the neighbour was a restricted one, which
referred only to members of one's own ethnic group and religion. In the parable of the Good Samaritan, in particular, Jesus
extended the understanding of neighbourliness and mutual forgiveness, to include everyone, even enemies.

In the Lord's Prayer, having said 'Forgive us our debts, as we
also have forgiven our debtors', Jesus went on to add, 'For if you
forgive others their trespasses, your heavenly Father will also
forgive you; but if you do not forgive others, neither will your
Father forgive your trespasses' (Mt 6:14). On another occasion,
Jesus said in similar vein: 'Do not judge and you will not be
judged; do not condemn, and you will not be condemned.
Forgive and you will be forgiven … for the measure you give (to
others) will be the measure you will get back (from God)' (Lk
6:36-39). At the end of the parable of the Unforgiving Servant,
the man who failed to show mercy was severely punished, and
Jesus commented: 'This is how my heavenly Father will treat
each of you unless you forgive your brother or sister from your
heart' (Mt 18:35).

The other New Testament writings echo these sentiments.
For example, in Col 3:13 we read: 'Bear with one another, forgive
each other if one has a complaint against another. The Lord has

forgiven you, you must do the same.' In Eph 3:32 the inspired
author says: 'Be generous to one another, sympathetic, forgiving
each other as readily as God forgave you in Christ.' Finally, St
James warned: 'For judgement will be without mercy to anyone
who has shown no mercy; mercy triumphs over judgement' (Jas
2:13).

Down the centuries, wise people have reiterated this vital
teaching. For instance, in 1751, Samuel Johnson wrote in the
Christmas edition of *The Rambler*: 'On him who hopes to be forgiven, it is indispensably required that he forgive. It is therefore
superfluous to urge any other motive. On this great duty eternity
is suspended; and to him that refuses to practise it, the throne of
mercy is inaccessible, and the Saviour of the world has been
born in vain.'

When we are consciously aware of hurts and their associated
negative feelings, we need to make the decision, with God's
help, to forgive others as we ourselves have been forgiven.
There is no grace we could ask for that could be more in accord
with the will of God. And as St John assured us: 'This is the confidence we have in approaching God: that if we ask anything according to his will, he hears us. And if we know that he hears us
– whatever we ask – we know that we have what we asked of
him' (1 Jn 5:14-15).

34 Indignant Compassion

There are many accounts of Jesus' healings in the gospels. One of the shortest is to be found in Mk 1:40-42. It describes how 'a man suffering from a virulent skin disease' came to Jesus. Presumably, he was sore and itchy. Emotionally it was embarrassing because it was so noticeable and off-putting. Socially, it was isolating because he was ritually unclean and people feared that his ailment might be contagious. So they avoided him. As a result the sick man felt he didn't fully belong.

No wonder he said to Jesus: 'If you are willing, you can cleanse me.' The man had faith, but it was hesitant. Intellectually he had no doubt that Jesus had the power to heal, but he wasn't emotionally convinced that Jesus wanted to heal him of his particular complaint, at that particular time.

Jesus empathised with the man in an understanding way. In an earlier version of Mark's gospel, the text said that he was angry. He wasn't angry with the leper, but rather with the disease. It implies that he was opposed to it because it had dared to disfigure the life of a precious child of God. Not surprisingly, Jesus had a strong desire to rid the man of his disease. I suspect that he realised that his indignant compassion was shared by his Father. In other words, he was being authorised to reach out and heal the man. As Jesus testified: 'By himself the Son can do nothing; he can do only what he sees the Father doing' (Jn 5:19).

As a result, Jesus said to the man, 'I am willing.' This was an inspired and inspiring word of prophecy. I'm quite sure that it transformed the man's hesitant faith into trust of the expectant kind. As St Paul said: 'Faith comes from hearing, and that means, hearing the word of Christ' (Rom 10:17). He had heard that living word and so he had no more doubts. It would be fulfilled because Is 55:11 promises that God's word does not return to God without achieving the purpose for which it was sent. Then we are told that Jesus 'stretched out his hand, touched him and said to him ... be cleansed. And at once the skin disease left him and he was healed.'

When we are hurting either physically, emotionally or socially, we need to come to Jesus in the same way. Like the man in the story, we acknowledge that Jesus can heal, but we may not be sure whether he wants to heal us of our particular distress, at this particular time. Instead of looking at Jesus from the point of view of our suffering, we need to look at our suffering from the point of view of our relationship with the Lord. He has compassion for us, while opposing our ailment, and ultimately wanting us to be rid of it. We wait for a revelation of God's will. Does the Lord want to heal us now, or sometime in the future? We pray inwardly, 'Only say the word and your servant shall be healed' (Lk 7:7).

God's word can come in number of ways such as a scripture verse that jumps alive into the heart, a moving sermon, an inspiring testimony, or a powerful inward conviction which is prompted by the Spirit. Then the Lord can bless us with divine power, either through a sacrament such as the anointing of the sick or the Eucharist, the ministry of another Christian, or by the direct action of the Holy Spirit, as we say, 'be it done unto me according to your word' (Lk 1:38).

35 Misery and Mercy

The story about the woman caught in adultery (Jn 8:1-11) was not in the original version of the gospel. This episode, reminiscent of others recounted in the synoptics, was accepted as inspired by the church. It was inserted into the text in the third century.

The Pharisees are out to trap Jesus. The woman has been caught in the act of adultery. In terms of strict justice, the situation is clear. She was guilty of the offence, and Deut 22:23-24 stipulated that, as a married woman, she should be stoned to death. However, Roman law did not allow the Jews to execute a person for religious reasons. So they asked Jesus what should they do. If he said, 'Stone her in accordance with the law' he would have been disobeying civil law and denying his own teachings on divine mercy (cf Jn 3:17; 12:47). If, on the other hand, he said: 'Don't stone her' he would have been contradicting precepts of scripture.

In the event, with wisdom characteristic of Solomon of old, Jesus changed the whole focus of the debate by saying: 'Let him who is without sin among you be the first to throw a stone at her.' In other words, if anyone present is innocent of sin, if he has never lusted after a woman in his heart (cf Mt 5:27ff) let him be the first to dispense justice. One by one, beginning with the eldest, all the men slinked away because, all of them had to acknowledge their own guilty secrets. Jesus and the woman were left facing one another. As St Augustine observed, she was the personification of *miseria* i.e. misery, while he was the personification of *misercordia* i.e. mercy.

Measured against his own criterion of sinlessness, Jesus had a right to stone the woman. But he didn't exercise that right. In Jn 8:10 we are told that he asked: 'Has no one condemned you?' She said, 'No one Lord.' And Jesus said, 'Neither do I condemn you; go and do not sin again.' What wonderful, liberating words. Later on, they were to find an echo in Rom 8:1: 'There is now no condemnation for those who are in Christ Jesus.' In other words, they are declared not guilty and acquitted, and free from punishment. How should we respond to this good news? In Lk 6:36-37 Jesus says that we should: 'Be merciful, just as your Father is merciful. Do not judge, and you will not be judged. Do not condemn, and you will not be condemned. Forgive, and you will be forgiven.'

Before his death, Pope Paul VI told Fr John Magee, now bishop of Cloyne, how he had been deeply influenced by the two words, misery and mercy, in St Augustine's commentary on Jn 8:1-8. 'Always, in all of us,' he said, 'there is a tension between my misery and God's mercy. The whole spiritual life of all of us lies between these two poles. If I open myself to the action of God and the Holy Spirit and let them do with me what they will, then my tension becomes joyous and I feel within myself a greater desire to come to him and receive his mercy; more than ever I recognise the need to be forgiven, to receive the gift of mercy. Then I feel the need to say thanks, and so my whole life becomes a thanksgiving, a Eucharist to God because he has saved me, redeemed me, drawn me to himself in love. It is not anything I have done in my life that saves me, but God's mercy.'

36 Was Jesus a Hasidim?

As you know, there were many groups in Palestine during our Lord's life and ministry. Among them were the Sadducees, Pharisees, Scribes, Zealots and Essenes. However, there was another group who are rarely mentioned in commentaries on the scriptures. They were known as the Hasidim, a word that was derived from the Hebrew *hesed*, meaning 'loving kindness.' They were holy men who were noted for their strict way of living and poverty. They had a saying, 'What is mine is yours, and what is yours is yours.' They are mainly remembered because of their ability to perform healings and miracles.

There were a number of these holy men living in Palestine around the same time as Jesus. The names and deeds of a few of them have come down to us. Firstly, there was Honi, the Circle-Maker. Like the prophet Elijah before him, he was able to pray effectively for rain. There was also Hanina ben Dosa. He was from a village twelve miles from Nazareth. He once told his daughter to put vinegar into a lamp. He said that when the oil ran out, 'he who commanded oil to burn will also command the vinegar to burn.' On another occasion he was bitten by a poisonous lizard. It was the reptile who died! He said to those present, 'See my children, it is not the lizard that kills, but sin.' The Hasidim had a characteristic saying, 'He whose actions exceed his wisdom, his wisdom shall endure; but he whose wisdom exceeds his actions, his wisdom shall not endure.'

We know that when Jesus was baptised in the Jordan, he was not only filled with the Holy Spirit, he also received many charisms, i.e. gifts of the Spirit, including an ability, reminiscent of the Hasidim, to perform deeds of power such as healings, exorcisms and miracles. Clearly, he shared their belief that such deeds spoke more eloquently than mere words. For example, when John the Baptist sent messengers to Jesus to ask whether he was the promised messiah or not, Jesus replied like a typical Hasidim: 'Go back and report to John what you hear and see: The blind receive sight, the lame walk, those who have leprosy are cured, the deaf hear, the dead are raised, and the good news is preached to the poor' Mt 11:4-5.

Modern day charismatics would maintain that Jesus wanted his disciples to continue his ministry, including his deeds of power. They can point to a number of texts to support their belief, including the following. 'I tell you the truth, anyone who has faith in me will do what I have been doing. He will do even greater things than these, because I am going to the Father. And I will do whatever you ask in my name, so that the Son may bring glory to the Father' (Jn 14:12-13). In 1 Cor 12:8-10, St Paul mentions some of the charismatic gifts that can be granted to Christian believers, such as faith to move mountains, healings, and miracle working. As St Paul said: 'The kingdom of God is not a matter of talk but of power' (1 Cor 4:20). The Hasidim, like Jesus, would have wholeheartedly agreed.

Perhaps Pope Paul VI had something like this in mind when he said in 1974: 'How wonderful it would be if the Lord would pour out the charisms in increased abundance, in order to make the church fruitful, beautiful and marvellous, and to enable it to win the attention and astonishment of the profane and secularised world.' Amen to that. So, 'let us earnestly desire the spiritual gifts' (1 Cor 14:1).

37 A Biblical Mantra

It is thought that John Cassian lived between 360 and 435 AD. As a young man he joined a monastery in Bethlehem. Later he spent time in Egypt studying monastic life there. Finally, he travelled to the West and founded two monasteries near Marseilles in present day France. During that time he published two books. One of them was entitled *The Institutes*. It contained Cassian's rules for monastic life. The second was entitled *The Conferences*. It recounted Cassian's conversations with the leaders of Eastern monasticism. This book became very influential in the Middle Ages. For about a thousand years it was read, on a regular basis basis, in Western monasteries. One of its best known conferences was Cassian's tenth, which mainly dealt with the use of mantras in prayer. Centuries later, its teaching had a big influence on the use of the Jesus Prayer in Eastern Orthodoxy, and the use of centring prayer in contemporary Catholicism.

In the course of his talk, Cassian told his monks that he would give them a prayer formula that would enable them to get very close to God. Then he said that this formula was given to him by a number of the most esteemed monks in the East. They only shared it with a very few people who were truly anxious to know the best way of getting close to God in prayer. Cassian said that if they wanted to be ever mindful of the Lord, they should say the following words: 'O God, come to my aid, O Lord make haste to help me' (Ps 70:1).

He went on to observe: 'This verse has rightly been selected from the whole bible for this purpose. It fits every mood of human nature, every temptation, every circumstance. It contains an invocation of God, a humble confession of faith, a reverent watchfulness, a meditation on our frailty, a confidence in God's answer, an assurance of his ever-present support. The person who continuously invokes God as his or her protector, is aware that he is always at hand. The formula contains a fervent charity, a fearful contemplation of the devil's power, and a regard for the defender's help which alone can relieve the belea-

guered soul from the devil's siege by day or night. Souls sunk in
apathy, worry or melancholy of any kind, find the cure for their
despair in this verse, which shows them that God watches over
their struggles and prayers. It warns souls that are happy in
their spiritual progress that they should avoid complacency, as-
suring them that only with God's protection can they keep what
they have won; teaching them not merely to ask for divine help,
but to ask it speedily.'

I find Cassian's contention, a very striking one. In many
ways, the verse he proposes for repetition as a mantra, does indeed encapsulate something of the spiritual essence of the Old
and New Testaments. It highlights the fact that as finite creatures, we ultimately depend on God's providential plan and
provision for everything, for our existence, talents, and for the
countless gifts and graces we receive. As a result, I find that in all
kinds of circumstances, whether good or bad, I can repeatedly
recite the scripture verse recommended by Cassian.

A thought. If you were to choose one single verse from the
whole bible, which would sum up your experience of Christian
spirituality, what would it be? Why would you single it out as
your key verse? If you have chosen such a line, why not learn it
off by heart. Then repeat it as your prayer mantra, much as
Cassian suggests.

38 Power in Praise

Luke recounts a marvellous incident in Acts 16:16-34. As a result of an inspired vision, Paul had travelled from Asia to Philippi in Europe. There he preached the good news. But he was often interrupted by a young girl, who was oppressed by an evil spirit. 'This girl started following Paul and the rest of us and shouting, "Here are the servants of the Most High God; they have come to tell you how to be saved!" She did this day after day until Paul became exasperated and turned round and said to the spirit, "I order you in the name of Jesus Christ to leave that woman." The spirit went out of her then and there' (Acts 17:17-18). The girl's handlers were furious. They couldn't use her anymore to make money by means of her fortune-telling. So they had Paul and his companion Silas arrested, sentenced, flogged, and imprisoned.

What did the two disciples do? They had broken no law. As Roman citizens they shouldn't have been flogged. Yet they had been unjustly and harshly dealt with. Did they get angry and rant and rave at their oppressors? No. They were in great pain, and bound in a dark and dank inner prison. Did they feel sorry for themselves as people who had been victimised? Not a bit of it. They rejoiced to be found worthy to participate in the sufferings of Christ (cf 1 Pet 4:13). 'In the middle of the night Paul and Silas were praying and singing God's praises, while the other prisoners listened' (Acts 16:25).

When some people suffer, they magnify their problems by concentrating on them. As a result, they seem to get bigger and bigger, while God seems to get smaller and smaller in comparison. Others magnify the Lord by concentrating on the divine glory. As a result, the Lord seems to become greater and greater, while their problems seem to become lesser and lesser in comparison. So instead of magnifying our problems we should magnify the Lord. As someone has wisely said: 'if the outlook is bad try looking upwards.' That's what Paul and Silas did. They praised the risen Lord, no matter how much they had to endure in this valley of tears.

In doing this they were imitating the example of heroes of

faith in the Old Testament. For example, the three young men praised God in the fiery furnace. Instead of being burnt alive they were set free (cf Dan 3:24). Jonah praised God in the belly of the whale. Instead of being lost at sea he was coughed up on the shore of liberty (cf Jonah 2:9-10). When Paul and Silas praised the Lord, 'Suddenly there was an earthquake that shook the prison to its foundations. All the doors flew open and the chains fell from all the prisoners' (Acts 16:26). As it says in Ps 22:3-4: 'You are enthroned in the praises of your people. In you our fathers put their trust; they trusted and you delivered them.' In other words, unconditional praise of God delivers us from a spiritual point of view.

A suggestion. Think of two points. Firstly, what is the worst thing that has happened to you? Secondly, what is the worst thing you yourself have done? Instead of engaging in excessive self-reference as a result of either, tell God how you feel about them. Then try to forget about yourself by concentrating on the Lord by means of wholehearted praise of God. As many of us already know, if this is done in an unconditional way, it can have a salutary effect.

39 The Unknown God

A number of years ago, my brother and I visited Athens. Like tens of thousands of other tourists we climbed the Acropolis to see the ruins of the Parthenon. It is still a vivid reminder of the cultural glories of ancient Greece. When we descended from the rocky hill, we walked along a meandering path until we came to a large stone. On it was affixed a bronze plaque containing Greek writing. I recognised that it was the text of Paul's speech about the unknown God in Acts 17:16-34. Immediately a great wave of sadness came over me. In the distance I could see large numbers of people streaming up and down the pre-Christian Acropolis, whereas my brother and I were the only ones standing at the Areopagus where the good news had been preached for the first time in Athens. I sighed inwardly and said, 'Lord Jesus, 2000 years later, there are still so many people who do not seem to know you.'

Luke tells us that Athens was adorned with many statues. Among them was one which was dedicated to an unknown God. In some ways our postmodern society is similar. There are many people who, despite their spiritual desire for meaning, are convinced that the time of certainties is irrevocably past. All we can know are partial and provisional truths. As a result they are agnostic about the existence and attributes of God. And yet, consciously or unconsciously, their longings for transcendence continue to motivate them.

The philosopher Friedrich Nietzche (1844-1900) rejected the unsatisfactory forms of bourgeois belief current in his own day. Nevertheless, he articulated the secret aspirations of many people when he wrote these surprising words. 'Solitary, I lift my hands to you, to whom I fly, to whom in my heart's deepest depth I have consecrated a ritual altar which continually recalls your voice to me. On it glow, deeply inscribed, the words: to the unknown God. His am I. ... I try to flee, yet he compels me back into his service. I will to know you unknown one, you who seize me deep in my soul, you who rove through my life like a storm, you, inconceivable, are kin to me! I will to know you, even serve you.'

If St Paul were alive today, he would wholeheartedly respond to aspirations such as these. We know from his time in Athens that his approach had a number of typical characteristics. Firstly, he was familiar with the local culture, its religion, philosophy and art forms. Secondly, he proclaimed the good news about the existence of God and the saving death and resurrection of Jesus by moving from the known to the unknown. This he did without watering down his beliefs. Thirdly, he relied on the power of the Holy Spirit to bring about conversions. As he said: 'My message and my preaching were not with wise and persuasive words, but with a demonstration of the Spirit's power' (1 Cor 2:4). No wonder the Pope John Paul has said: 'Paul's speech in the Areopagus is a model of inculturation.' In other words, Paul expressed the unchanging truth of the gospel in a way that the people of that particular culture would be able to relate to, understand and accept.

It provides a reliable blueprint of how we can conduct the new evangelisation, called for by the Pope, by relating the gospel message to our pluralistic, urban, postmodern culture. We can do so by means of such things as Life in the Spirit Seminars, Alpha and Power to Change courses, and Cursillo weekends.

40 Faithfulness

There is a popular saying: 'The road to hell is paved with good intentions.' It acknowledges the fact that we live in a world of broken promises where people often let us down, either as a result of ill-will, or weakness. Psychologist Erik Erickson has argued that we first begin to realise this fact in early childhood, and that it is often confirmed by events as we grow older. Consequently, our capacity to trust in other people is compromised and our ability to form intimate relationships, of a committed kind, is undermined.

In Gal 5:22 St Paul wrote: 'But the fruit of the Spirit is love, joy, peace, patience, kindness, goodness, faith, gentleness, self-control.' In modern bibles the Greek word for faith is variously translated as 'faithfulness,' 'fidelity,' and 'trustfulness.' Dependability as a fruit of the Spirit is the expression of Christian character, the outcome of the heart's graced union with the Lord Jesus who himself was faithful.

The bible tells us: 'If we are faithless, God will remain faithful, for he cannot disown himself' (2 Tim 2:13). As a result, the promises of the Lord are completely trustworthy. The word used in Hebrew of the Old Testament is *aman*, which means 'to be faithful'. For example, in Deut 7:9 we read: 'Know therefore that the Lord your God is God; he is the faithful (*aman*) God, keeping his covenant of love to a thousand generations of those who love him and keep his commands.' This sentiment is echoed repeatedly in the New Testament. Here the Greek *pistos* is used. It too means 'faithful'. For instance, in 2 Thess 3:3 Paul says: 'The Lord is faithful (*pistos*), and he will strengthen and protect you from the evil one,' and again, 'Let us hold unswervingly to the hope we profess, for he who promised is faithful (*pistos*)' (Heb 10:23).

The word Amen, which is mentioned 100 times in the gospels, is derived from Hebrew and means to 'confirm, support, establish, or verify'. It is rooted in the notion that God's word is reliable because it originates in the One who is uniquely dependable, trustworthy, constant and faithful. So when Jesus said 'Amen I say to you...' one could paraphrase his words to mean, 'As God is reliable, you can place your confidence in what I am about to say.' For our part, when we respond to such things as the divine promises, liturgical prayers and reception of sacraments with the word 'Amen' we are saying in effect: 'As God is reliable, let it done unto me according to the divine will.'

In the Christian life we are called, with the Spirit's help, to be for others what God is for us. We are to bear witness to God's faithfulness by keeping our promises, both great and small. A few years ago I read a book with the provocative title, *Can Anyone Say Forever?* Its Jesuit author, John C Haughey, wondered whether modern Christians were capable, any longer, of making life-long commitments such as those involved in marriage, the priesthood and religious life. Judging by the rising divorce rate and the numbers of people seeking annulments and dispensations from solemn vows, the answer often seems to be no. However I'm convinced that when we rely on God's help, we can keep our promises. As Paul says: 'God is faithful; he will not let you be tempted beyond what you can bear. But when you are tempted, he will also provide a way out so that you can stand up under it' (1 Cor 10:13). Today's young people need credible mirrors of divine faithfulness.

41 The Bible of Creation

There are two great bibles, the scriptures and creation. Italian scientist, Galileo Galilei (1564-1642) once remarked that, properly understood, they cannot contradict one another, because they both proceed from the same God. In this reflection we will look at the way in which creation can give us intimations of the existence and attributes of its Creator. As St Thomas Aquinas stated: 'The nature of man requires that he be led to the invisible by visible things. Therefore, the invisible things of God must be made manifest to man by the things that are visible.' So, just as the moon reflects the light of a sun we cannot see, so the natural world reflects the glory of a God we cannot know directly.

The bible makes this point over and over again. For example, in Wis 13:5 we read: 'From the greatness and beauty of created things comes a corresponding perception of their creator.' Again in 2 Mac 7:28, the mother of the seven Maccabee brothers says to one them: 'I implore you, my child, look at the earth and sky and everything in them, and consider how God made them out of what did not exist, and that human beings came into existence in the same way.' That point finds an echo in Ps 19:1-2 which says: 'The heavens declare the glory of God; the skies proclaim the work of his hands. Day after day they pour forth speech; night after night they display knowledge.' St Paul reiterates this point when he writes: 'For since the creation of the world God's invisible qualities – his eternal power and divine nature – have been clearly seen, being understood from what has been made, so that men are without excuse' (Rom 1:20).

For Christians, therefore, creation is the sacrament or icon of God. A hymn in the Divine Office rightly observes: 'The Father gives his children the wonder of the world, in which his power and glory, like banners are unfurled.' This has two interrelated consequences. Firstly, like Jesus, we should prayerfully contemplate the myriad beauty of natural things, such as the lilies of the field (cf Mt 6:28). We do so in Hopkins's belief that 'the world is charged with the grandeur of God.'

Secondly, our contemplation can be augmented by the findings of great scientists whose painstaking investigations reveal just how great and marvellous the cosmos really is. Let's look at only one mind-boggling example. There are about one thousand million stars in our galaxy. However, the Milky Way is only one of billions of galaxies. A light year is the distance that light travels, in 12 months, at a little over 186,000 miles a second. If one looks at the part of the universe that is 15 billion light years wide, it contains an estimated 2000 billion, billion stars! Despite this unimaginably great number, space is largely empty. In a typical galaxy, the stars are twenty million, million miles apart. Space is as crowded with stars, as the surface of the Pacific Ocean would be if two grains of pollen were put floating on its surface!

Just as works of art reflect the minds and hearts of those that created them, so the wonders of creation bear witness to the beautiful mind and heart of the One who brought them into being. As Cardinal Newman wrote: 'There is only one thought greater than that of the universe and that is the thought of its maker.' So besides reading the scriptures, also read the book of nature, with the help of modern science. It too was written by the same Author.

42 Scripture on Dreams

In the ancient world people saw dreams as a way of receiving revelation from God. In the modern world people see dreams as a way of getting in touch with the contents of the personal and collective unconscious. I suspect that there is truth in both points of view. When one reads what the bible has to say about dreams one gets the distinct impression that it expresses two apparently contradictory attitudes.

On the positive side, there is the belief that dreams are the dark speech of the Spirit. There are a number of texts that support this point of view. In Job 33:14-15 we read: 'For God does speak – now one way, now another – though man may not perceive it. In a dream, in a vision of the night, when deep sleep falls on men as they slumber in their beds.' In Num 12:6 the Lord says: 'Listen to my words: When a prophet of the Lord is among you, I reveal myself to him in visions, I speak to him in dreams.'

There are many Old and New Testament examples of people receiving guidance in dreams. Gen 31:24 tells us that: 'God came to Laban the Aramean in a dream at night and said to him, "Be careful not to say anything to Jacob, either good or bad."' In I Kgs 3:5 we are told that: 'At Gibeon the Lord appeared to Solomon during the night in a dream, and God said, "Ask for whatever you want me to give you."' In the gospels, Joseph, the husband of Mary repeatedly received guidance in dreams. They concerned his marriage to Mary (Mt 1:20), the exile of the Holy family in Egypt (Mt 2:13), their return (Mt 2:19) and the decision to settle in Galilee (Mt 2:22). Later in Matthew's gospel we are told how Pilate's wife said to her husband during the trial of Jesus, 'Have nothing to do with that innocent man because in a dream last night I suffered much on account of him' (Mt 27:19). The early Christians also received revelation in dreams. For example, St Paul was led to go to Europe as a result of one (cf Acts 16:6-11).

In the bible, a special gift is needed to interpret the religious meaning of dreams. When the chosen people dreamt, they could interpret the meaning themselves. But when pagans had similar dreams they needed gifted Jews to discern their meaning. For example, early in the bible two men say: 'We both had dreams ... but there is no one to interpret them.' Then Joseph said to them, 'Do not interpretations belong to God? Tell me your dreams' (Gen 40:8).

The bible also warns against taking dreams too seriously. For instance, it says: 'Much dreaming and many words are meaningless' (Eccl 5:7), and 'dream are folly, and like a woman in travail the mind has fancies ... for dreams have deceived many, and those who have put their trust in them have come to grief' (Sir 34:5-7). Although the scriptures are skeptical about the value of natural dreams, they do accept that God can use them in order to fulfil the divine purposes. 'Unless they are sent from the Most High as a visitation, do not give your mind to them' (Sir 34:6).

Nowadays, we would be more open to the fact that natural dreams can help a person to grow in self-awareness by highlighting such things as unacknowledged inner conflicts, forgotten memories and feelings, and one's need for the healing touch of God. So if you are troubled ask God, before you go to sleep, to bless you with a religious dream.

43 Testing

Sir 2:1 warns: 'My child, when you come to serve the Lord, prepare yourself for testing.' There are a number of images of such testing in the bible. Firstly, there is the notion of the difficult journey. When the Israelites left Egypt, they meandered for years in desert regions. They had promised to be faithful to the God who had delivered them from slavery. Theoretical loyalty is one thing, the reality, another. Deut 8:2-3 explained: 'The Lord your God has led you these forty years in the wilderness, in order to humble you, testing you to know what was in your heart, whether or not you would keep his commandments.' In the event the people failed. Remember how they broke the first commandment by worshipping the golden calf.

Secondly, there is the notion of refining gold. When the precious metal is taken from the earth it contains many chemical impurities which might not be obvious from its appearance. But when the metal is melted, the impurities rise to the surface. When the dross is removed the purified gold is allowed to cool. With this image in mind, 1 Pet 1:7 says: 'the genuiness of your faith, being more precious than gold, though perishable, is tested by fire.'

Thirdly, there is an image of winnowing; of separating the useless chaff from the precious grains of wheat. Jesus had this in mind when he spoke to the apostles before passion week. He said: 'Simon, Simon, listen! Satan has demanded to sift all of you like wheat, but I have prayed for you that your own faith may not fail; and you, when once you have turned back, strengthen your brothers' (Lk 22:31). There are a number of points worth making about this remarkable verse. It shows that God sometimes allows the devil to test us by means of temptation. It presumes that Peter will fail, due to lack of self-awareness and humble dependence on God. Jesus prays that when he slips on the banana skin of weakness he will not despair, like Judas, but will trust in the Lord by acknowledging his desperate need for the Holy Spirit which would be poured out at Pentecost.

All of us experience predictable and unpredictable crises.

They test our fidelity, faith and fortitude. We can expect to undergo a predictable psychological crisis about every ten years, or so. It can last for anything up to three years. Then there are unpredictable crises such as bereavement, ill health, relationship difficulties, and the like. As luck would have it, sometimes predictable and unpredictable crises occur at the same time. They are often associated with emotional depression and spiritual desolation. We feel far from God, and are subject to all kinds of nagging temptations.

If we are humble and dependant on the Lord, during times of testing, we will receive the grace to resist temptation. We will be able to resist doubts and the inclination to engage in escapist activities, e.g. by drinking too much, or getting involved in inappropriate sexual behaviour. As St Paul assured us: 'No temptation has seized you except what is common to man. And God is faithful; he will not let you be tempted beyond what you can bear. But when you are tempted, he will also provide a way out so that you can stand up under it' (1 Cor 10:13). If perchance we fall, God will not only forgive our sin, the Lord will subsequently strengthen us by the Spirit. Then, we will be able to say, 'O happy fault, O necessary sin, that won for me such self-awareness and liberating grace.'

44 Divine Providence

On the day Princess Diana died I heard a priest paraphrase one of the beatitudes. He said: 'Blessed are those who know their need of God.' Jesus was well aware that we live in a dangerous and threatening world where we have to confront our neediness in many ways. Firstly, there is the problem of material poverty. For example, many people in the third world live on the margins of existence. They have to depend on such things as the vagaries of the weather, governmental agencies and the generosity of others. Secondly, in the developed world there is what Mother Teresa referred to as the famine of the heart. It's mainly due to a lack of understanding love. It is often experienced in the form of such things as isolation, loneliness, depression, neurosis, addiction and obsessions of different kinds.

When faced with the uncertainties of life Jesus encouraged his disciples to trust in the providence or foresight of God. He believed that God has a benevolent plan for each of our lives. He agreed with what Jeremiah had written: 'For surely I know the plans I have for you, says the Lord, plans for your welfare and not for harm, to give you a future and a hope' (Jer 29:11). That plan is expressed in two interrelated ways. There is our overall vocation in life, whether married or single. Within that context we need to be guided by the Spirit on a day to day basis (cf Gal 5:18). As Cardinal Newman wrote: 'Lead kindly light amid the encircling gloom ... I do not ask to see the distant scene, one step enough for me.'

Jesus taught that, besides having a plan for our lives, God provides for us in our needs. Divine provision is experienced in two ways. Firstly, there is internal help in the form of our natural talents and God-given graces. As Paul says: 'It is God who is at work in you, enabling you both to will and to work for his good pleasure' (Phil 2:13). God also provides for us in external ways. As Jesus said: 'You must not set your hearts on things to eat and drink; you must not worry. It is the Gentiles of this world who set their hearts on all these things. Your Father well knows you need them. No, set your hearts on his kingdom , and these other things will be given you as well' (Lk 12:30). The Lord will usually do this through secondary causes, such as coincidences and the kindness and generosity of other people.

What happens when we fail to carry out God's plan for us? Fortunately, God has alternative plans B, C, D etc. Each one is as good, if not better than the last. That was is evident in the story of Joseph and his brothers. They were merciless when they sold their gifted sibling into slavery. Years later they had to travel to Egypt during a time of famine. Unbeknown to them Joseph was the man they had to deal with. Having revealed his identity to the brothers he said: 'Come close to me.' When they had done so, he said, 'I am your brother Joseph, the one you sold into Egypt! And now, do not be distressed and do not be angry with yourselves for selling me here, because it was to save lives that God sent me ahead of you' (Gen 45:4-5). Ironically, their treachery was used as the springboard of future blessing! Such are the mysterious ways of providence. As St Paul observed: 'in everything God works for good with those who love him' (Rom 8:28).

45 Christ Within

The presence of Christ within Christians is affirmed in a number of scripture texts, e.g. 'Remain in me,' said Jesus, 'and I will remain in you' (Jn 15:4). St Paul said: 'The life I live now is not my own; Christ is living in me' (Gal 2:20). St Peter asserted that we are 'sharers of the divine nature' (2 Pet 1:4).

Paradoxically, the more I relate to others, the more I discover and relate to my own deepest self. If you reflect on your relationships you will become aware of the fact that we grow in self-awareness through our struggle to grow in intimacy. It confronts us with the limits of such things as our trust, generosity, patience and our ability to receive.

As I contemplate God the Father, in and through his Son, I get to know my own divine potential, my Christ-self. Pope John Paul II has said: 'God is present in the intimacy of man's being, in his mind, conscience and heart.' When I'm filled with the Spirit, I have the felt sense, as Thomas Merton expressed it, that: 'My deepest realisation of who I am is – I am one loved by Christ … The depths of my identity is in the centre of my being where I am loved by God.' Christ's biography, therefore, is my potential autobiography. Par 521 of the *Catechism of the Catholic Church* describes the profound effects of the divine indwelling which began with the sacraments of baptism and confirmation: 'Christ enables us to live in him all that he himself lived, and he lives it in us.'

In his *The Life and Kingdom of Jesus in Christian Souls*, St John Eudes (1601-1688) drew out an important implication of this spiritual truth. He began by quoting a well known Pauline text: 'I make up what is lacking in the sufferings of Jesus Christ for the sake of his body the church' (Col 1:24). He then went on to observe that what Paul says about our sufferings can be extended to all our other actions as well. He said that any true Christian, who is united to Christ by his grace, continues and fulfils, through all the actions that he or she carries out in the spirit of Christ, the actions that Jesus Christ performed during his brief life on earth.

So when a Christian prays, she continues and fulfils the prayer that Jesus Christ offered on earth. Whenever she works, she continues and fulfils the laborious efforts of Jesus Christ. Whenever she relates to her neighbour in a spirit of unconditional love, then she continues and fulfils the relational life of Jesus Christ. Whenever he eats or rests in a Christian manner, he continues and fulfils the subjection that Jesus Christ wished to have to these necessities. The same can be said of any other action that is carried out in a Christian manner.

When you are about to embark on different tasks you will often run into the buffers of your own natural weakness and limitations. Say to Jesus: 'Lord, the good I wish to do, I cannot do, but you are living out the mysteries of your life in me. Enable me by the Spirit that animated your ministry, to continue and fulfil that same ministry in my own life. Give me the ability to do this task, and I thank you that you are achieving even more than I can ask or imagine through the power of your Spirit at work within me.' When you affirm the divine indwelling in this way, you will have the conviction that your efforts will be blessed and fruitful.

46 Friendship in the Old Testament

Friendship was esteemed in the Greco-Roman world. Writers such as Pythagoras, Plato, Aristotle and Cicero wrote eloquently about it. Friendship was also highly valued in the Old Testament. For example there are many passages, especially in the wisdom literature, which describe false and true friendships. They may have been influenced by Greek thinking following Alexander's conquests in the fourth century BC.

Prov 17:17 observes: 'A friend loves at all times.' In Sir 6:14-17 we read: 'Faithful friends are a sturdy shelter: whoever finds one has found a treasure. Faithful friends are beyond price; no amount can balance their worth. Faithful friends are a life-saving medicine; and those who fear the Lord will find them. Those who fear the Lord direct their friendship aright, for as they are, so are their neighbours also.' In Eccl 4:9-10 we read: 'Two are better than one, because they have a good return for their work: If one falls down, his friend can help him up. But pity the man who falls and has no one to help him up!'

This ideal of friendship was epitomised by the relationship between Ruth and Naomi, and David and Jonathan. In Ruth 1:16, Naomi's daughter-in-law says: 'Don't urge me to leave you or to turn back from you. Where you go I will go, and where you stay I will stay. Your people will be my people and your God my God.' In 1 Sam 18:1-5 we are told that 'Jonathan became one spirit with David and loved him as himself ... he swore eternal friendship for him. He took off the robe he was wearing and gave it to David, together with his armour and also his sword and his belt.' This archetypal relationship prefigured relationships in the early Christian church where the community of believers would be 'one in mind and heart' and would 'have all things in common' (Acts 4:32).

The Old Testament offers a good deal of sage advice about friendship. It recognises that some people form friendships for the sake of some selfish advantage or pleasure. For example in Sir 37:4 we read: 'A false friend will share your joys, but in time of trouble stands afar off.' Some time later we are warned: 'there are friends who are friends in name only.' So the scriptures counsel caution when making friends. A time of probation is needed to see if the potential friend will be trustworthy. 'When you gain a friend,' says Ben Sirach, 'first test him, and be not too ready to trust him' (Sir 6:7). In another place he says: 'He who betrays a secret cannot be trusted' (Sir 27:16). But if, and when, he or she proves worthy of loyal friendship, 'every friend declares his friendship' (Sir 37:1).

The bible acknowledges that friends will let one another down, but these conflicts can usually be resolved within the bonds of friendship. However, it warns that 'a wound can be bound up, and an insult forgiven, but he who betrays secrets does hopeless damage' (Sir 27:21). Later, we are told: 'A contemptuous insult, a confidence broken, or a treacherous attack will drive away any friend' (Sir 22:22). The notion of friend betraying friend is mentioned in Psalm 55:12-14. It anticipates in a poignant manner the way Judas would betray Jesus. 'If an enemy were insulting me,' says the psalmist, 'I could endure it; if a foe were raising himself against me, I could hide from him. But it is you, a man like myself, my companion, my close friend, with whom I once enjoyed sweet fellowship as we walked with the throng at the house of God.'

47 Friendship in the New Testament

Jesus was a God-intoxicated man. All his earthly relationships were subordinated to this primary one. He left his family and only acknowledged them in so far as they did the will of God. He said: 'Whoever does what God wants him to do is my brother, my sister my mother' (Mk 3:5). Although Jesus had nothing against sexual relationships, he renounced marriage for the sake of the kingdom. He said: 'In heaven there will be neither marriage nor giving in marriage' (Mt 22:30). It is striking, however, that Jesus formed intimate friendships in adult life. He was a friend of Lazarus, and possibly his sisters Mary and Martha. On one occasion his critics said that he was 'a friend of tax collectors and sinners' (Mt 11:19). Clearly, he was friendly with all of the apostles. He said to them, 'I have called you friends' (Jn 15:15). It would appear that Peter, James and John were his closest friends among the twelve. On special occasions such as the transfiguration (Mk 9:2), the raising of the daughter of Jairus (Mk 5:37) and the agony in Gethsemane (Mk 14:33), he took them with him.

What makes friendship different from other less intimate relationships, is the degree of self-disclosure involved. As he said: 'I have called you friends, for everything that I learned from my Father I have made known to you' (Jn 15:15). In other words, 'my intimate self is in union with God, and I have revealed the innermost secrets of that relationship to you.' St Ambrose commented: 'Christ provides us with the formula of friendship, namely: that we do the will of our friend, that we reveal to our friend whatever secrets we have in our hearts, and that we be aware of his secrets. For a friend hides nothing. If he is true, he pours forth his soul just as the Lord Jesus poured forth the mysteries of his Father.'

Jesus came to realise that his friends would never truly understand the intimate truths he revealed unless they received the Holy Spirit. It would lead them 'into all truth' (Jn 16:13). But he could only give them the Spirit by first yielding it up to his Father in death. Surely, that awareness was implicit in the words: 'Greater love has no one than this, that he lay down his life for his friends. You are my friends' (Jn 15:13-14).

The last words that Jesus spoke on the cross: 'Into your hands I commit my Spirit' (Lk 23:46) were not only the extreme expression of friendship love, they were a necessary prelude to Pentecost. On that fateful day, the Spirit was poured out upon the apostles. It was as if Jesus had walked through the walls of their bodies to live within them. As a result, they enjoyed a relationship of remarkable intimacy with their erstwhile friend. He was no longer the One who was with them in the body, but rather the Christ who was living in them by his Spirit. Through the action of the Spirit that searches 'the hidden depths of God', they had 'that mind which was in Christ Jesus' (1 Cor 2:10, 16).

Many of the saints have felt that just as friendship was important in the life of Jesus, so it can play an important role in our lives too. In fact, there is an intimate connection between our Christian friendships and friendship with Christ. As Jesus assured us: 'Where two or three come together in my name, (especially in friendship love) there am I with them' (Mt 18:20). Clearly, he who abides in friendship abides in God.

48 Sacred Time

There are two kinds of time, secular and sacred. They often intersect. Secular or chronological time is measured by clock, watch and calendar. It is unredeemed time, in which we experience our chronic problems. Sacred time is qualitative rather than quantitative. It is the mysterious point where the eternal now, of a timeless God, is experienced in our lives. It is redeemed time in which we can experience God's grace-filled intervention. It is also the time of crisis, a turning point for better or worse, which presents us with a decisive choice for or against God's liberating purposes. Both forms of time are evident in the bible.

In the scriptures God's time is mentioned on a number of occasions, notably when describing the birth, baptism, death, resurrection and second coming of Jesus. For example, when he began his preaching, it is significant that he said: 'The time has come. ... The kingdom of God is near. Repent and believe the good news!' (Mk 1:15). When Mary intimated that Jesus might change water to wine at the marriage feast of Cana, he declared that it wasn't God's plan for such a manifestation of divine glory. 'Dear woman,' he said, 'why do you involve me? ... My time has not yet come' (Jn 2:4). On another occasion the apostles asked if Jesus would be accompanying them to Jerusalem to celebrate the feast of tabernacles. He replied: 'You go to the feast. I am not yet going up to this feast, because for me the right time has not yet come' (Jn 7:8).

In each of these incidents, Jesus was referring to God's designated time, the occasion when the divine, redemptive purposes were to be accomplished. On one occasion Jesus spoke about the intersection of secular and sacred time when he said: 'When evening comes, you say, "It will be fair weather, for the sky is red," and in the morning, "Today it will be stormy, for the sky is red and overcast." You know how to interpret the appearance of the sky (in chronological time), but you cannot interpret the signs of the times (in sacred time)' (Mt 16:2-3).

Two important factors of time are implicit in the concept of sacred time, those of providence and revelation. The idea of divine providence asserts that our lives are neither governed by blind chance, or inexorable fate. God has a saving plan for the world and for each one of us. The nuances of that foresight are experienced in and through events. We need the gift of discernment of spirits (1 Cor 12:10), which was so evident in the life of Jesus, to recognise the 'signs of the times'. These sacred moments are also occasions of revelation when the Lord manifests the divine presence, word and will to us in a number of possible ways such as intuitions, dreams, visions, prophetic awareness, inspiring scripture verses etc. Thus we are 'guided by the Spirit' (Gal 5:18) in such a way that we can co-operate with God's saving purposes. These notions are implicit in the following verses: 'From now on I will tell you of new things, of hidden things unknown to you. They are created now, and not long ago; you have not heard of them before today. So you cannot say, "Yes, I knew of them"' (Is 48:6-7).

Christians have one foot in time, another in eternity. They long for the second coming of Jesus at an indeterminate time in the future. As he said: 'It is not for you to know the times or dates the Father has set by his own authority' (Acts 1:7). In response we pray: Come, Lord Jesus!

49 Miracle Working

When the Greek of 1 Cor 12: 10 is literally translated into English it says, to some is given 'operations of works of power'. However, most translators use the shorter phrase 'the working of miracles.' The word 'miracle' comes from the Latin *miraculum*, meaning 'a wonder'. From a religious point of view a miracle is a supernatural manifestation of divine power which goes beyond the laws of nature, as we currently understand them, in such a way as to evoke religious awe and wonder in those who witness them.

We know that some of the great heroes of faith in the Old Testament performed miracles. For instance Elijah raised a dead man, cured Naaman the leper, multiplied food and had God consume his sacrifice on Mount Carmel. In the New Testament, Jesus performed even greater miracles. In Jn 14:12, he also promised that all those who believed in him would perform even more impressive miracles. In the Acts we see that 'many signs and wonders were done among the people by the hands of the apostles' (Acts 5:12).

Modern Catholics have been familiar with the working of miracles in three ways. Firstly, they are associated with great saints who performed them during their lives and after their deaths. For example, during his life, St Francis of Paola (1416-1507) of Calabria in Italy, was probably the greatest miracle worker the church has ever seen. When saints die, one or two miracles are required for their canonisation. But, when St Charbel Makhlouf (1828-1898), a Maronite hermit from the Lebanon, was declared a saint in 1977, Pope Paul VI revealed that more first class miracles were submitted in support of his cause than for any other saint in history.

Secondly, miracles are associated with shrines like Lourdes. Its medical bureau applies criteria which were established in the 1700s by Pope Benedict XIV. He stipulated that in order to declare that a healing was miraculous it must be established that the disease was serious; that there was objective proof of its existence; that other treatments had failed; and that the cure was rapid, lasting and inexplicable from a scientific point of view.

Thirdly, there is the gift of miracle working. In 1 Cor 12:10 Paul says that in the Christian community it is possible that people could be gifted with the ability to perform occasional miracles. To understand his thinking correctly it is important to see this gift in the context of his theology of the community as the Body of Christ. It is called to proclaim the good news of the outpouring of God's unconditional mercy and love and to demonstrate its presence. It does so, not only by means of loving relationships, deeds of mercy and action for justice, but in a specially striking way by means of deeds of power, such as healing, exorcism and miracle working. Like the performance of the other deeds of power, miracle working, whether in the form of inexplicable healing or changes in nature, depends upon the charism of expectant faith (cf Mk 11:22-24; 1 Cor 12:9). It is evoked in the heart by a revelation of God's purposes. Whereas a healing assists and accelerates the body's natural potential for recovery, a miraculous healing goes well beyond what science thinks the body is capable of achieving.

Up to recently, many educated people found it hard to believe in miracles. Happily, a new scientific worldview is emerging. It maintains that nature is an open system. God can act in a miraculous way by exploiting the potential of matter when it is influenced by the Holy Spirit as a result of the co-operation of faith-filled human beings.

50 Spiritual Intuition

Jesus seemed to be able to read people's hearts and to predict future events. For instance, he appeared to know all about Nathaniel although he had never met him before (Jn 1:48), and he was able to tell the Samaritan woman that she hadn't one husband, but five (Jn 4:18). In the New Testament church some of the believers were granted the same gift. For example, we are told that on one occasion the prophet Agabus: 'stood up and through the Spirit predicted that a severe famine would spread over the entire Roman world. This happened during the reign of Claudius' (Acts 11:28).

The most important New Testament reference to the word of knowledge is to be found in 1 Cor 12:8 where St Paul says: 'To one there is given through the Spirit ... message of knowledge by means of the ... Spirit.' Speaking of the gift of knowledge, scripture scholar, Gordon Fee, says that it can be understood in two ways. Firstly, there is the 'utterance of knowledge', which usually takes the form of inspired teaching. Secondly, there is 'a supernatural endowment of knowledge, factual information that could not otherwise have been known without the Spirit's aid, such as frequently occurs in the prophetic tradition.' I was interested to see that Anglican bishop David Pytches endorses Fee's second interpretation. He states that the word of knowledge is a 'supernatural revelation of facts about a person or situation, which is not learned through the efforts of the natural mind, but is a fragment of knowledge freely given by God, disclosing the truth which the Spirit wishes to be made known concerning a particular person or situation.' Many modern scripture scholars would agree with St Thomas Aquinas's belief that, as a form of private revelation, the word of knowledge is a prophetic gift.

Over the years I have found that that 'words of knowledge' can be received in different forms, such as an intuition, an inner word, or an imaginative picture. However they are received they can be invaluable in different ministry situations. Firstly, in the sacrament of reconciliation some priests will occasionally known a penitent's secret sins. This knowledge enables them to help the person to make a good confession. Secondly, the Lord can guide intercessory prayer by means of a 'word of knowledge'. At a prayer meeting in Northern Ireland, for example, I heard a woman praying about a very specific trouble spot in Belfast. The next day we found out from the newspaper that at the very time she was praying, a car bomb had failed to go off in the exact location she had been concerned about. Thirdly, those who pray for inner healing are sometimes led by a 'word of knowledge' to focus on a repressed memory. A man who was suffering from claustrophobia went to a priest I know. After a few minutes of prayer he said 'You were nearly drowned when you were three.' Immediately, the man recalled such a forgotten incident. Following a brief prayer, his phobia disappeared completely. Fourthly, as the ministry of Kathryn Kuhlman demonstrated, words of knowledge are sometimes granted to those praying for physical cures, particularly at healing services.

Not only do the four kinds of 'words of knowledge' guide people, they also evoke the gift of unhesitating faith that moves mountains. As St Paul tells us in Rom 10:17, faith is evoked by hearing God's inspiring word. Because of the ever present danger of illusions and false inspirations, it is important to check in order to ascertain whether private revelations, one's own or those of others, truly come from God (cf 1 Jn 4:1).

51 The Unforgivable Sin

Although the New Testament stresses over and over again that God is willing to forgive any sin, there is a shocking and disturbing passage in the synoptic gospels about an unforgivable sin. Jesus said in Mt 12:32: 'Anyone who speaks a word against the Son of Man will be forgiven, but anyone who speaks against the Holy Spirit will not be forgiven, either in this age or in the age to come' (cf Mk 3:28; Lk 12:10).

The context of Jesus' saying throws light on its meaning. The Lord had been exorcising people of evil spirits. The Pharisees accused him of doing so by the power of Beelzebul. As Jesus pointed out, it was absurd to maintain that the devil was driving out the devil. In actual fact it was by the Spirit's power that deliverance was accomplished. But to attribute a deed to the devil that was clearly performed by the Spirit was blasphemous. As the same Spirit is necessary for repentance, how could a person feel sorry for sin if he or she had denied the very Spirit that makes such sorrow possible?

In his encyclical *Lord and Giver of Life* (1986) Pope John Paul II commented on this notion of the sin against the Holy Spirit. Firstly, he said by way of explanation: 'Blasphemy does not properly consist in offending against the Holy Spirit in words; it consists rather in the refusal to accept the salvation which God offers to man through the Holy Spirit, working through the power of the Cross.' Secondly, he added: 'Blasphemy against the Holy Spirit is the sin committed by the person who claims to have a "right to persist in evil" – in any sin at all – and who thus rejects redemption.' It is interesting to note that the Pope does not give concrete examples of what he means by a totally permissive lifestyle. Is he referring to people of no religion who have devoted themselves to a life of immorality, or to people who, in spite of knowing God and experiencing the power of the Spirit, have freely chosen to abandon their faith and to ignore the commandments? I suspect it is the latter.

Then John Paul seems to say that while God is willing to forgive every sin, even the sin against the Holy Spirit, that same sin irrevocably prevents them from availing of that forgiveness. The Pope says: 'The blasphemy against the Holy Spirit consists precisely in the radical refusal to accept that forgiveness ... it does not allow one to escape from one's self-imposed imprisonment and open oneself to the divine sources of the purification of conscience and the remission of sins.' The *Catechism of the Catholic Church* endorses this point of view when it says in par 1864: 'There are no limits to the mercy of God, but anyone who deliberately refuses to accept his mercy by repenting, rejects the forgiveness of his sins and the salvation offered by the Holy Spirit. Such hardness of heart can lead to final impenitence and eternal loss.'

This notion of the unforgivable sin is mentioned, in one way or another, in a number of other texts such as 1 Jn 5:16-17; Heb 6:4-5; and Heb 10:26-27. It would probably be true to say that each of them can be properly interpreted, more or less, in the way that has been outlined. From what Jesus said it was clear that he revered the Holy Spirit, acknowledged its pre-eminent and indispensable role in repentance and salvation, and wanted us to be filled with the 'the Lord and giver of life'.

52 I Did it My Way

The book of Judges describes what happened after the death of Joshua and before the establishment of the Jewish monarchy. It recounts how Judges such as Gideon, Samson and Deborah provided charismatic leadership in Israel. Chapter two points out that there was a tendency towards infidelity among the people. 'Abandoning the Lord, the God of their fathers ... they followed the other gods of the various nations around them.' For example, Jgs 17:1-7 tells how Micah stole some silver from his mother. When he returned it, she was so happy that she had it melted down and made into an idol. Not surprisingly, there was also moral decline. For example, in Jgs 19:22-29 we are told how, in order to protect himself, a Levite gave his concubine to a group of Jewish men who had originally intended to sexually assault him. Instead, they savagely raped the unfortunate woman over and over again. Shortly, after her terrible ordeal she died. The last verse of the book, encapsulates the basic reason for such a widespread breakdown of faith and morals: 'There was no king in Israel; everyone did what was right in his own eyes' Jgs 21:25.

It has struck me on a number of occasions that this verse has considerable relevance in contemporary Ireland where, in Yeats's words, it often seems that: 'things fall apart; the centre cannot hold ... the best lack all conviction.' Like other Western societies, ours is a postmodern, secular one. It maintains that, rather than being an objective fact, all our knowledge – including moral knowledge – is at best partial and provisional. Nothing is absolutely certain. As a result there is a growing tendency to make ethics a matter of private opinion and choice. There is considerable evidence to show how many people, in public and private life, have been rewriting the commandments to suit themselves.

Over the past 20 years, three European Values Systems Studies have indicated how many people adopt an *à la carte* approach to morality by picking and choosing what seems right to them. They do so in the name of personal conscience, believing that there aren't any really reliable, objective standards, for judging right from wrong. For example, a well known Irish pop singer reflected the views of many when he confessed in the *Sunday Independent*, 12 May 2002: 'I have my faith, I don't go to church now or have a priest dictate how to live my life. I read the bible and do things my own way.' This privatisation of morality is evident in society in general. In recent years there has been a significant increase in the numbers having intercourse before marriage, living together, using artificial forms of contraception, engaging in gay sex, and procuring abortions. Their theme tune could be Frank Sinatra's, 'I did it my way!'

When he wrote *Splendour of the Truth* in 1993, Pope John Paul II stated that we need to restore our reverence for God's sovereign authority as the heavenly King. The Lord has revealed the moral truths which are reliably taught by the church. In our search for ethical guidelines we should make use of the light of reason and revealed truth. Together they tell us that there are acts, such as euthanasia, child sex abuse, torture, rape, injustice, pornography and genocide which are always intrinsically wrong. Intentions, circumstances or consequences can never make them right. Wouldn't it be great, in the years to come, if we experienced such Christian revival and renewal, that we could say: 'In these days, Christ is the King in Ireland, and everyone does what is right in his eyes.'

53 Slander

In the letter of James there is a striking passage which talks about the way in which we can sin by means of what we say. A modern paraphrase translates it as follows: 'By our speech we can ruin the world, turn harmony to chaos, throw mud on a reputation, send the whole world up in smoke and go up in smoke with it, smoke right from the pit of hell. This is scary. You can tame a tiger, but you can't tame the tongue' (Jas 3:5-8). One of the main ways in which the tongue can cause harm is by spreading negative stories about other people. They may be confidential secrets, rumours, or downright falsehoods. One way or another, they can deprive people of their right to a good reputation and thereby cause immense pain to the victims, their families and friends. I know this from personal experience. A number of years ago, a rumour was circulated which maintained that I had left the priesthood and married. It even spread to Australia. There was no truth in it whatsoever. I found it hurtful and felt that it undermined both my good name and the work I was doing. But there was very little I could do to counteract it.

In Lev 19:16 we read: 'Do not go about spreading slander among your people', and in Lev 25:17 'Do not take advantage of each other, (i.e. by means of telling tales) but fear your God.' In 1 Sam 21-22, there is a story which describes the fatal damage that can be caused by spreading defamatory information about a person. A Jew called Doeg betrayed David and Ahimelech, a man who had helped David in a time of need. He told king Saul that he had reason to believe that the two were plotting against him. He interpreted Ahimelech's kind and innocent action of giving David food and the sword of Goliath, as proof positive that subversive action was being planned. This slanderous story subsequently led to the murder of Ahimelech and many priests.

There is a non-biblical tale which also illustrates the harm that can be done by irresponsible and malicious speech. A man spread lies about his rabbi. Sometime later he realised the harm he had done. He went to the rabbi and asked his forgiveness. He said he would do anything to make amends. The rabbi said to him: 'Take a feather pillow, cut it open, and scatter the contents to the winds.' The man thought this was a strange request, but it was a simple one, and he performed it gladly. When he returned to tell the rabbi that he had carried out his instructions, he said, 'Now go and gather the feathers. Because you can no more make amends for the damage your words have done than you can collect the feathers.'

It is interesting to note that the words slander and scandal are derived from the Greek *skandalon*. It originally referred to the spring of a trap, on which the bait was placed. It would snap into action when the trap was activated. In like manner, people become ensnared by the negative stories that are disseminated about them. Needless to say, true Christians avoid saying anything that would take away from another person's reputation, by drawing attention to anything that might detract from his or her character. To do otherwise would offend against the silver rule of Tob 4:15: 'Do to no one what you would not want done to you', and the teaching of Jas 4:11 which states: 'Brothers and sisters, do not slander one another.'

54 Hospitality

Our national tourism board is known as Bord Fáilte, i.e. the Board of Welcomes. In modern, prosperous, fast-moving Ireland, it is easy to get the impression that instead of extending the traditional 100,000 welcomes, many of our citizens are seeking a 100,000 ways of engaging in rip-offs. Instead of showing hospitality to visitors, some people seek to exploit them in one way or another, e.g. by overcharging and poor service. Apart from being bad for business and our national reputation, such a lack of hospitality is downright unethical.

Over and over again, the bible stresses the importance of hospitality. For example, as Gen 18:1-15 indicates, Abraham was the archetypal host when he invited strangers into his house, washed their feet, prepared fresh meat, had Sarah bake bread, and later accompanied them as they left. They turned out to be angels, i.e. the messengers of God. Apparently, the present practice in some Arab countries is something similar. A traveller may sit at the door of a perfect stranger and smoke his pipe until the householder welcomes him with an evening meal. He may also stay a number of days without questions being asked. He may then depart with a simple 'God be with you' as his only payment.

In the New Testament it is much the same. When one reads the gospels it is noticeable that Jesus highlights the importance of welcoming different types of people, especially the poor. Those who give them a good reception are not only welcoming fellow human beings, they are welcoming Christ himself, and through him, his heavenly Father. Speaking about kids Jesus said: 'Whoever welcomes one of these little children in my name welcomes me; and whoever welcomes me does not welcome me but the one who sent me' (Mk 9:37). Referring to evangelists, he said: 'I tell you the truth, whoever accepts anyone I send accepts me; and whoever accepts me accepts the one who sent me' (Jn 13:20). In another place the Lord stated: 'Anyone who receives a prophet because he is a prophet will receive a prophet's reward, and anyone who receives a righteous man because he is a righteous man will receive a righteous man's reward. And if anyone gives even a cup of cold water to one of these little ones because he is my disciple, I tell you the truth, he will certainly not lose his reward' (Mt 10:41-42). In Mt 25:40 we are told why this is so: 'I tell you the truth, whatever you did for one of the least of these brothers or sisters of mine, you did for me.'

The later New Testament writings echo this attitude when they say: 'Share with God's people who are in need. Practice hospitality' (Rom 12:13); and again 'Offer hospitality to one another without grumbling' (1 Pet 4:9). There are many examples of such hospitality. For instance, Acts 18:26, tells us that when Aquila and Priscilla heard Paul preaching in a local synagogue they invited him to their home and shared their Christian faith with him. In words that echo back to Abraham's experience, Heb 13:2 adds: 'Do not forget to entertain strangers, for by so doing some people have entertained angels (i.e. the messengers of the Lord) without knowing it.'

Hopefully, the modern, prosperous Ireland will continue to be hospitable and welcoming rather than selfish and exploitative. As Daniel O Connell, one of our greatest Christian patriots once said: 'The hospitality of an Irishman is not the running account of posted and ledgered courtesies, as in other countries; it springs, like all his qualities … directly from his heart.'

55 Witnessing to Jesus

The ancient account of Polycarp's martyrdom is truly inspiring. He was brought before a Roman governor who said to him 'Revile your Christ.' Polycarp's reply was, 'Eighty and six years have I served him, and he has done me no wrong. How then can I blaspheme my King and my Saviour? … I am a Christian, and if you want to know the meaning of Christianity, you have only to name a day and give me a hearing.' Shortly afterwards, Polycarp was burnt at the stake because of his faithfulness. His heroic witness was the kind of fidelity Jesus had in mind when he said: 'Whoever acknowledges me before men, I will also acknowledge him before my Father in heaven. But whoever disowns me before men, I will disown him before my Father in heaven' (Mt 10:32).

Instead of concentrating on what scripture says about Jesus, this reflection will focus on what some well known historical figures have said about him. Surprisingly, Napoleon Bonaparte, wrote: 'Everything in Christ astonishes me. His spirit overawes me, and his will confounds me. Between him, and whoever else in the world, there is no possible term of comparison … I search in vain in history to find the similar to Jesus Christ, or anything which can approach the gospel. Neither history, nor humanity, nor the ages, nor nature, offer anything with which I am able to compare it or to explain it. Here everything is extraordinary. The more I consider the gospel the more I am assured that there is nothing there which is not beyond the march of events, and above the human mind.'

Russian novelist, Fydor Dostoyevsky acknowledged: 'I believe there is nothing lovelier, deeper, more sympathetic and more perfect than the Saviour; I say to myself with jealous love that not only is there no one else like him, but there could be no one. I would say even more. If anyone could prove to me that Christ is outside the truth, and if the truth really did exclude Christ, I should prefer to stay with Christ and not with the truth. There is in the world only one figure of absolute beauty: Christ.'

Albert Einstein, a Jewish scientist, said: 'As a child I received instruction both in the bible and in the talmud. I am a Jew, but I am enthralled by the luminous figure of the Nazarene ... No one can read the gospels without feeling the actual presence of Jesus. His personality pulsates in every word. No myth is filled with such life.'

Mohandas Gandhi, a Hindu politician, stated: 'What then does Jesus mean to me? To me, he was one of the greatest teachers humanity has ever had. To his believers he was God's only begotten son ... Is all the grandeur of his teaching and of his doctrine to be forbidden to me? I cannot believe so. To me it implies a spiritual birth. My interpretation, in other words, is that in Jesus' own life is the key to his nearness to God; that he expressed as, as no other could, the spirit and will of God.'

On one occasion Jesus asked the apostles: 'Who do you say I am?' (Mt 16:15). He addresses the same question to you and me, not just in the quiet safety of our private thoughts, but in more demanding, public ways. We need to be willing to openly confess our faith in him, with firm conviction, without equivocation or compromise. As 1 Pet 3:15 says: 'Always be prepared to give an answer to everyone who asks you to give the reason for the hope that you have. But do this with gentleness and respect.'

56 Stormy seas

When I was a teenager I attended an uncle's marriage. I can remember my late father saying a few words at the reception. He compared marriage to a journey by sea. Sometimes the waters are calm, at others, stormy. But, with God's help, the couple can make it together to the harbour of marital fulfillment. Happily, my uncle and aunt did just that right up to the time of their deaths.

In the bible there are a number of marvellous accounts of epic sea journeys such as Jonah's vicissitudes on the way to Niniveh (Jon 1:4-15), the tempest described in Ps 107:23-30, the storm on the sea of Galilee in Mt 8:23-27, and St Paul's scary trip from Adramyttium, a seaport in Asia Minor, to Rome. It is described in Acts 27. Read the accounts for yourself. While they can be interpreted in strictly historical terms, they can also be understood as metaphors. The boat can be seen as the Christian community which is buffeted by the winds and waves of adversity. However, the church learns to cope by relying solely on the Lord. As Ps 89:8-9 puts it: 'O Lord God Almighty ... you rule over the surging sea; when its waves mount up, you still them.'

Recently, when I was reading about Paul's eventful maritime adventure I couldn't help thinking that it has a lot to say to the contemporary church which is being battered by temptation, infidelity and scandal. As Pope John Paul II warned, prophetically, in 1979: 'Your country seems in a sense to be living again the temptations of Christ: Ireland is being asked to prefer the kingdoms of the world and their splendour to the kingdom of God. Satan, the tempter, the adversary of Christ, will use all his might and all his deceptions to win Ireland for the way of the world ... Now is the time of testing for Ireland. This generation is once more a generation of decision.'

In Paul's case, the ship's passengers survived a period of violent storms because Paul received a prophetic revelation from the Lord. As he said: 'Last night an angel of the God, whose I am and whom I serve, stood beside me and said, "Do not be afraid, Paul. You must stand trial before Caesar; and God has graciously given you the lives of all who sail with you." So keep up your courage, men, for I have faith in God that it will happen just as he told me' (Acts 27:23-25). When they heard this word, the captain and the Roman centurion, together with everyone else, believed and acted as Paul had instructed. They were willing to jettison everything, even their food and lifeboat. All they could do then, was to rely solely on the God of the word. As a result, they all survived as Paul had promised.

During the present stormy crisis in the church we have to listen to God. I believe that the Lord has been speaking words of warning and guidance over the past 25 years. For example, on Easter Monday, 1976, a prophecy was spoken in the presence of Paul VI, in St Peter's Basilica. It said that days of darkness, testing, and purification were coming upon the church. Afterwards, there would follow the greatest age of evangelisation the world has ever seen. Right now we are experiencing the days of darkness. It is merely a painful prelude to great things to come. Meantime, we have to get rid of all the worldly props and supports that are separating us from complete and utter dependence on, and fidelity to the Lord.

57 Giving in Order to Receive

Many years ago I saw a TV programme about a Northern Ireland preacher who was appealing for funds to build a large church in Belfast. He began by quoting a foundational Christian verse. You have often seen references to it on placards at sporting events. It reads, 'God so loved the world that he gave his only Son, that whoever believes in him may not die but may have eternal life' (Jn 3:16). Instead of dwelling on the mystery of the incarnation, the Northern evangelist with an American twang said, 'My dear people, see how God the Father was willing to give us his greatest gift, the gift of Jesus his beloved Son. You should be willing to be like God by being generous in your financial giving.' He then went on to expound what is sometimes known as the prosperity gospel. The greater people's generosity, the greater would be the material blessings they would receive in return. Then he went on to cite examples of individuals and families who had given what little they had to the church. Soon afterwards, he claimed, they had experienced a dramatic improvement in their financial fortunes. In giving they had received, just as Jesus had promised in Lk 6:38.

Although there was more than a kernel of truth in what this preacher said, I found it very off-putting. It seemed to distort the true spiritual meaning of the scriptures in order to serve his own questionable ends. It is true that God is extraordinarily generous to each one of us and that we should try to reflect that generosity in our dealings with others. But surely one shouldn't do so in order to be blessed in material ways. Generosity isn't genuine if it has strings attached. Jesus became human because it would benefit us, and not because it would benefit him. As he said: 'Freely you have received, freely give' (Mt 10:8).

In any case the underlying assumptions of the prosperity gospel are highly questionable. I suspect that they are the result of a number of factors. Firstly, some Calvinists, with their doctrine of predestination, are inclined to believe, like the Old Testament Jews, that material prosperity is an outward sign of divine favour. Secondly, a sizeable number of American evan-

gelical Protestants are inclined to think that their capitalist way
of life is virtually synonymous with true Christianity. Instead of
critiquing the assumptions of their materialistic culture in the
light of gospel values, they sometimes seem to endorse those
values by a selective and arbitrary use of scripture texts.

It is interesting to note that they conveniently ignore the op-
tion for the poor, and the needy. More often than not, they fail to
help them in material ways, or to identify and change the unjust
and oppressive structures that aggravate their poverty. The
truth is, Jesus choose to become poor among the poor. As St Paul
wrote, 'For you know the grace of our Lord Jesus Christ, that
though he was rich, yet for your sakes he became poor, so that
you through his poverty might become rich' (2 Cor 8:9). When
the apostle talks about becoming rich, he means rich in grace,
not necessarily in financial terms. As Jesus told the rich young
man, if he wanted to become perfect he should 'go, sell your
possessions and give to the poor, and you will have treasure in
heaven. Then come, follow me' (Mt 19:21).

Nowadays, many Catholics argue with good reason that we
can only interpret the gospels reliably when we are poor in spirit,
relate empathically with the poor and oppressed, and do what
we can to liberate them.

58 Spiritual Freedom

Surely all peoples, no matter what cultures they belong to, long to enjoy inner and outer freedom. The French Revolution, which has had such an influence on the Western world, proclaimed the ideal of liberty, while the American Declaration of Independence asserted that people are endowed with unalienable rights, among them liberty. Spiritual people have pointed out that we need to be free from inner and outer constraints in order to be free for worthwhile choices, such as the decision to worship the living God in spirit and truth.

It is not surprising to find that the Bible has a lot to say about human freedom. We will focus on just one point. Jn 8:31-32 reads: 'Then Jesus said to the Jews who had believed in him, "If you make my word your home, you will indeed be my disciples; and you will come to know the truth, and the truth will set you free".' A home is the place where one is nurtured physically, emotionally and spiritually. It is a *locus* of primordial relationships, redolent with memories, where one truly belongs.

It is interesting to note that rather than saying: 'if my word finds a home in you' Jesus says, 'if you make my word your home'. In other words if you always find shelter and nurturance in what Jesus says, if you hold fast to his teachings and live by them, you will come to know the revealed truth of God. This echoes the Socratic notion that truth can only be revealed to those who love it and put it into practice. Jesus may have had this practical understanding in mind when he prayed: 'Sanctify them in the truth; your word is truth' (Jn 17:17). God's word protects believers from the illusions and false inspirations of the evil One, who seeks to enslave people to wrongdoing. As Jesus said: 'Very truly I tell you, everyone who commits sin is a slave to sin. The slave does not have a permanent place in the household; the son has a place there forever. So if the Son makes you free, you will be free indeed' (Jn 8:34-36).

The parable of the Prodigal Son is a wonderful illustration of how a person can move from slavery to sin, to the freedom of the children of God. He does so by coming to his senses and simul-

137

taneously making his home in the liberating word and house of his compassionate father. When his dad gives him shoes, they are a sign of his new found freedom and dignity because, unlike slaves, only beloved members of the household could wear footwear indoors.

As St Paul knew from personal experience: 'For freedom Christ has set us free. Stand firm, therefore, and do not submit again to a yoke of slavery' (Gal 5:1). How do we go about this? St Paul makes two suggestions in Gal 5:13: 'Do not use your freedom as an opportunity for self-indulgence.' As the *Catechism of the Catholic Church* reminds us in par 2342, mastering self-indulgence: 'is a long and exacting work ... It presupposes renewed effort at all stages of life.' But 2 Tim 1:7 assures us that it is possible because Christians have received a spirit of self-control. Paradoxically, Paul concludes: 'Through love become slaves to one another.' In other words, put the towel of service around your waist (cf Jn 13:4) and do for others what you would have them do for you (cf Mt 7:12; Lk 6:31), without counting the cost or expecting anything in return. When the hand is conformed in this way to a loving heart, a person has achieved true Christian freedom.

59 Jesus our Scapegoat

The Old Testament notion of the scapegoat was a curious ritual associated with the Day of Atonement. Two goats that had been chosen by lot were involved. Lev 16:21-23 tells us what the priest was supposed to do: 'and laying hands upon its head, he should confess over it the sins of the people of Israel. He shall lay all their sins upon the head of the goat and send it into the desert … and so the goat shall carry all the sins of the people into a land where no one lives'. Meantime the second goat was sacrificed.

Later in the Old Testament the prophet Isaiah pointed, in a prophetic way, to Jesus as the definitive scapegoat. The sins of the people would be laid on him, he would carry them on their behalf so that they might be forgiven. 'The Lord has laid on him the iniquity of us all … the righteous one my servant, shall make many righteous' (Is 53:5, 11). St Paul echoed this sentiment when he wrote: 'For our sake God made him to be sin who knows no sin, so that in him we might become the righteousness of God' (2 Cor 5:21).

However, Isaiah went beyond the teaching of the Book of Leviticus which had merely stressed the scapegoat's ability to carry away the sins of the people. The suffering servant on the other hand would also bear the mysterious sufferings and diseases of the people that they might experience healing of mind and body. 'Surely he has borne our infirmities and carried our diseases, ' wrote the prophet, 'and we have been healed by his bruises' (Is 52:25). Later, writing about Jesus, St Peter echoed these words when he wrote: 'Through his bruises you have been healed' (1 Pet 2:25).

Some time ago when I was reflecting on this mystery of salvation I recalled an occasion in my childhood when I got a nasty wound in my leg. I had been climbing a tree. A branch broke and a piece of wood stuck into my thigh muscle. As soon as I got home my mother removed it and dressed the wound. Some time later, my father, a veterinary surgeon, made a poultice which was designed to draw out the infection while disinfecting the damaged tissues. In the event it was very effective.

What occurred to me was that Christ, our scapegoat, is the poultice of God. He not only enfolded our wounds on the cross, he continues to do so. It is moving to think that Christ, the innocent One, was in a sense willing to absorb the evil of our sin and suffering into himself. On Calvary this unparalleled act of compassion was symbolised by the darkness that enveloped him as his life blood ebbed away: 'It was now about noon, and darkness came over the whole land until three in the afternoon' (Lk 23:44). It was as if Christ absorbed into himself all that alienated us from God and personal wholeness, as he sank firstly into the dark night of the soul and secondly into the shadowy dwelling place of the living dead. As he did so he offered us the wonderful balm of his forgiveness and healing.

There is a second lesson we can learn from Jesus the scapegoat. As his followers, we Christians need to act as the poultice of the world. We need to be willing to absorb the sin and hurts of society into ourselves, in a compassionate non-reactive way. Meanwhile, with the Spirit's help, we can offer those who attack and accuse us, in different ways, the forgiveness and healing love of Christ.

60 Sacred Music

Sometimes when I listen to sacred music my spirit soars with such a strong sense of exultant praise that I feel like shouting and dancing for joy. On other occasions I am moved to tears by the sheer beauty and emotional power of music such as Goretski's *Symphony of Sorrowful Songs*. Unfortunately, although it means so much to me, I cannot read notation or play an instrument. I don't normally sing and when I do, I don't sing normally. Nevertheless, I cannot imagine life without all kinds of music. Its melodies, rhythms and sound textures put me in touch with the deeper things of life.

You won't be surprised to know that music played an important role in the lives of biblical people. Because they were forbidden to have any paintings or statues depicting the Lord, they concentrated on musical forms of expression. The Jews sang on occasions such as marriages, funerals, coronations, marching into battle and at their religious services. They were often accompanied by stringed instruments such as lyres and harps, wind instruments such as horns and trumpets, and percussion instruments such as bells and hand drums. The final psalm says: 'Praise him with fanfare of trumpet, praise him with harp and lyre, praise him with tambourines and dancing, praise him with strings and pipes, praise him with the clamour of cymbals, praise him with triumphant cymbals' (Ps 150:3-5). In another place the psalmist confirmed modern findings about the salutary effects of music when he said: 'with the harp I will solve my problem' (Ps 49:4).

Jesus sometimes referred to music. In the parable of the return of the Prodigal Son, he mentioned that when the elder brother came in from the fields 'he heard music and dancing' (Lk 15:25). It is interesting to note that the Greek word used here is *sumphonia*, from which the English word, 'symphony' is derived. It literally means 'sounding in unison.' Jesus also referred to music in Mt 11:17 when he said: 'We played the pipes for you, and you wouldn't dance; we sang dirges and you wouldn't be mourners.' We also have reason to believe that Jesus himself sang the sacred music of his people. In Mt 26:30 it says that 'when they (i.e. Jesus and the apostles) had sung a hymn, they went out to the Mount of Olives.' St Augustine once referred to the Lord as 'The royal singer of the psalms.'

Not surprisingly, sacred music was prevalent in the New Testament church. St Luke told us about the unjust imprisonment of two disciples in Philippi. 'About midnight, as Paul and Silas were praying and singing hymns of praise to God, the other prisoners were listening to them' (Acts 16:25). Later on, St Paul said that music had an important part to play in prayer meetings. 'When you meet together,' he said, 'each one has a hymn' (1 Cor 14:26). The author of Eph 5:19 added: 'Sing psalms and hymns and inspired songs among yourselves, singing and chanting to the Lord in your hearts.'

People today do much the same. For example, when I'm driving, I often sing at the top of my voice in tongues, which is comprised of unknown words and melodies that are inspired by the Holy Spirit. It has been suggested that this kind of spontaneous music may have been the origin of Gregorian chant. One way or the other, St Augustine was correct when he wrote: 'One who sings well prays twice.' In doing so we prepare on earth to join the heavenly choirs in thunderous and unending praise, as they sing before the throne of God (cf Rev 14:2-3; 15:3).

61 Irrevocable Blessing

St Paul stated: 'God's gifts and call are irrevocable' (Rom 11:29). In other words, the Lord never withdraws the vocation and its accompanying graces that have been offered to people. When he said this, he had the Jews in mind. They were God's chosen people. God had made the covenant with them. The Messiah would be one of them, and through him all peoples would be blessed.

At first, Paul rejected Christ, but following his conversion he accepted him as his Lord and Saviour. However, it broke his heart to think that many of his co-religionists had failed to accept the Messiah. He confessed: 'I have great sorrow and unceasing anguish in my heart. For I would wish that I myself were accursed and cut off from Christ for the sake of my own people' (Rom 9:2-3). When one recalls how ardently Paul loved Jesus, this is a remarkable statement. But Paul believed that God loved the Jews even more passionately than he did. This led him to a number of convictions.

Firstly, God would use Jewish rejection of the Messiah as a providential means of blessing non-Jewish people. As he stated: 'through their stumbling salvation has come to the Gentiles' (Rom 11:11). Secondly, Paul believed that God would never reject his people or rescind the call or gifts that had been offered to them. As he stated: 'God has not rejected his people whom he foreknew' (Rom 11:2). Thirdly, Paul believed that, before Christ's second coming, the Jewish people would accept Jesus as their Messiah. He said: 'They have now been disobedient in order that, by the mercy shown to you, they too may now receive mercy' (Rom 11:31).

Arguably, these points can be extended to our own lives. All of us receive a call and associated graces from God. No matter how far we wander from the straight and narrow, where Christian faith and morals are concerned, the Lord will never revoke our call or withdraw its empowering graces. If, and when, we come to our senses and return to the Lord, we will be blessed as if we had never strayed.

I have great admiration for the late Kathryn Kuhlman (1908-

1976). As a young Protestant she experienced a vocation to become an evangelist. As she obeyed the call she found that she
had been richly blessed with a remarkable gift of healing. Some
years later, despite her own misgivings and the entreaties of
friends, she married a man who had abandoned his wife and
two children. Not surprisingly, her ministry went into decline.
Years later she acknowledged that she was living a lie. She said:
'I had come to the place in my life where I was ready to give up
everything – even my husband – and die. I said it out loud, "Dear
Jesus, I surrender all. I give it all to you."' When she returned to
ministry, she was more successful than ever and went on to become one of the greatest healers of the twentieth century. *Time*
magazine, went so far as to refer to her as 'a walking Lourdes'.

The same can be true in our own lives. The divine call and its
associated graces are irrevocable. Even if we are unfaithful, God
will remain faithful (cf 2 Tim 2:13). If we come to our senses and
return to the Lord, the graces associated with our vocation will
reassert themselves as strongly as ever. By the way, as Christians,
shouldn't we share Paul's love for the Jewish people by praying
regularly that increasing numbers of them will accept Jesus as
their promised Messiah?

62 The Bible on Booze

One of the downsides of the newfound prosperity in Ireland is a 40% increase in the consumption of alcohol in the 1990s. It is leading to all kinds of problems such as alcoholism, misdemeanors, higher suicide rates, car crashes, ill-health etc. In the light of these facts we can look at what the bible has to say about drinking.

The Jews of the Old and New Testaments drank wine. As a created thing, it was seen as being good in itself, a true gift of God. 'Wine gladdens the heart of man,' says Ps 104:15. Wine raises the spirits of those who are suffering so, 'let them drink and forget their poverty and remember their misery no more' advises Prov 31:7. Jesus changed water into wine at the marriage feast of Cana (Jn 2:1-11), which prefigured the mystical meaning he would give it at the last supper, when he declared: 'This is my blood of the covenant, which is poured out for many ... I tell you the truth, I will not drink again of the fruit of the vine until that day when I drink it anew in the kingdom of God' (Mk 14:24-25). In 1 Tim 5:23 Paul tells a young colleague about alcohol's medicinal properties: 'Stop drinking only water, and use a little wine because of your stomach and your frequent illnesses.' It would be true to say, therefore, that taken in reasonable quantities, wine is a blessing. As Sir 31:27 declares: 'Wine is very life to man if taken in moderation.'

However, the bible has a good deal to say about the evils that attend immoderate drinking. In Prov 23:29-35 we read: 'Who has woe? Who has sorrow? Who has strife? Who has complaints? Who has needless bruises? Who has bloodshot eyes? Those who linger over wine, who go to sample bowls of mixed wine. Do not gaze at wine when it is red, when it sparkles in the cup, when it goes down smoothly! In the end it bites like a snake and poisons like a viper. Your eyes will see strange sights and your mind imagine confusing things.' Scripture warns that heavy drinkers can act in an irreligious way: 'Woe to those who rise early in the morning to run after their drinks, who stay up late at night till they are inflamed with wine. They ... have no regard for the deeds of the Lord, no respect for the work of his hands' (Is 5:11-12). In another place it says that heavy drinking can lead to sexual impropriety (Hab 2:15). Ministerial effectiveness too, can be hampered by drunkenness: 'Priests and prophets stagger from beer and are befuddled with wine; they reel from beer, they stagger when seeing visions, they stumble when rendering decisions' (Is 28:7-8).

St Paul sees drunkenness as a sign that people are living from their natural, unredeemed selves, rather than their redeemed, spiritual personalities. In Gal 5:21 he says that drunkenness is sinful, and adds ominously: 'I warn you as I warned you before; those who do such things will not inherit the kingdom of God!' When Carl Jung was consulted by one of the founders of Alcoholics Anonymous, he explained that heavy drinkers are looking for ecstasy in the wrong place. Created things, such as spirits, are no substitute for the Holy Spirit. He concluded that only a genuine experience of God could rescue people from alcoholism, by enabling them to stand outside themselves in self-forgetful awareness of the divine. So, in the words of Paul: 'Do not get drunk on wine, which leads to debauchery. Instead, be filled with the Spirit' (Eph 5:18).

63 Childhood

There is a striking phrase which says: 'Childhood lasts a lifetime.' From a negative point of view we can say that if a child suffers from emotional, physical or sexual abuse, the knock-on effects can continue to influence the person throughout adult life. Modern psychology has thrown a lot of light on this dynamic. For example, a woman marries. She has a conscious intention of making a success of her relationship. But her resolve is unconsciously subverted by the psychological baggage she brings from childhood. Negative feelings surface, to do with the deprivations and hurts of her early years. Conflicts ensue. They become so acrimonious that the love which led her to marry progressively dies. Clearly, if a person was traumatised as a child, s/he needs counselling, a spirit of forgiveness, and repeated prayer for inner healing.

On the other hand, if a child experiences constant and dependable love from its parents, it will probably grow to be trusting, secure, self-assured, empathetic and self-forgetful. The knock-on effects will influence the person for the rest of his or her life. If, for example, a man marries with the intention of being committed to his wife, he will be sustained by the psychological strengths he brings to the relationship from his childhood.

It has occurred to me that because he was like us in all things but sin (cf Heb 4:15), Jesus was deeply influenced by his childhood experiences. Catholic psychiatrist, Jack Dominian, has suggested in *One Like Us* that, rather than being motivated by an unacknowledged sense of deprivation and inferiority, that could be traced back to his childhood, Jesus was at ease with everyone, including the poor, outcasts and sinners (cf Mt 11:19). This was so precisely because he was at ease with himself as a result of his loving upbringing by Mary and Joseph (cf Lk 2:40).

It has also occurred to me that Jesus' happy upbringing profoundly effected his attitudes to childhood and children. At a time when kids were ignored, his outlook was different. There is an incident which encapsulates this point. 'People were bringing little children to Jesus to have him touch them, but the disciples rebuked them. When Jesus noticed this, he was indignant. He said to them, "Let the little children come to me, and do not hinder them, for the kingdom of God belongs to such as these. I tell you the truth, anyone who will not receive the kingdom of God like a little child will never enter it." And he took the children in his arms, put his hands on them and blessed them' (Mk 10:13-16).

St Thérèse of Lisieux was particularly touched by the words: 'I tell you the truth, unless you change and become like little children, you will never enter the kingdom of heaven. Therefore, whoever humbles himself like this child is the greatest in the kingdom of heaven' (Mt 18:3-4). As a result of her prayerful reflection on Christ's teaching, Thérèse advocated the little way of spiritual childhood. 'To be a child,' she explained, 'is to recognise our nothingness, to expect everything from God as a little child expects everything from its father; it is to be disquieted about nothing ... To be little is not attributing to oneself the virtues that one practices, believing oneself capable of anything, but to recognise that God places this treasure in the hands of his little child to be used when necessary; but it always remains God's treasure. Finally, it is not to become discouraged over one's faults, for children fall often, but they are too little to hurt themselves very much.' For Christians, childhood lasts for eternity.

64 Spiritual Intelligence

At the beginning of the twentieth century the notion of Intelligence Quotient (IQ) tests was introduced. They were intended to measure how quickly and comprehensively a person could engage in insightful, abstract thinking. Since then a psychologist called Howard Gardner has suggested that there are multiple forms of intelligence which can embrace such activities as linguistic, logical-mathematical, spatial, musical and inter-personal intelligence. More recently there has been talk of spiritual intelligence. It refers to an ability that enables people to experience a simultaneous sense of belonging to the universe, other people, their deepest selves and God. In the light of this sense of connection with the divine mystery, in and through all human relationships, they seem to have an intuitive sense of how spiritual values should impinge on everyday decision making.

The bible esteems wisdom, or spiritual intelligence, very highly. In 1 Kgs 3:7-12 and 2 Chron 1:2-14, we are told how Solomon went to a shrine at Gibeon, four miles northwest of Jerusalem. There he had a religious dream in which God said to him. 'Ask what I should give you.' The king replied, 'Give your servant an understanding mind to govern your people, able to discern between good and evil.' The Lord was so pleased by Solomon's single minded desire for spiritual intelligence that he promised him: 'Because you have not asked for yourself long life or riches, or for the life of your enemies, but have asked for yourself understanding to discern what is right, I now do according to your word. Indeed I give you a wise and discerning mind.' In 1 Kgs 4:29-30 we are told that: 'God gave Solomon very great wisdom, discernment and breadth of understanding as vast as the sand on the seashore.'

When the bible speaks of wisdom, such as Solomon's, it refers principally to a spirit of discernment, which is the fruit of intimate relationship with God. It enables the gifted person to distinguish good from evil in everyday life. The wisdom of Solomon was so great that we are told how the queen Sheba, came a long distance to visit him. 'Solomon answered all her questions; there was nothing hidden from Solomon that he could not explain to her' (1 Kgs 10:3). It is interesting to note that Jesus referred to Sheba's visit, 'She came from the ends of the earth to listen to the wisdom of Solomon, and see, something greater than Solomon is here!' (Mt 12:42). As Paul was later to testify: 'Christ is the wisdom of God' (1 Cor 1:24).

We need the gift of wisdom (cf Is 11:2), the kind of spiritual intelligence which enables us, like Jesus, to discern, amid the illusions and false inspirations of everyday life, which decisions and actions are inspired by the Spirit of God and which are not. As the author of Col 1:9-10 testified: 'we have not ceased praying for you and asking that you may be filled with that knowledge of God's will in all spiritual wisdom and understanding, so that you may lead lives worthy of the Lord, fully pleasing to him.'

Many people ask for this kind of spiritual intelligence by saying a prayer which has been attributed to Cardinal Mercier: 'Come, O Holy Spirit, soul of my soul, I adore you. Enlighten me, guide me, strengthen and console me. Show me what to do and help me to do it. Give me your inspirations. I promise to submit myself to all that you desire of me and to accept all that you permit to happen to me. Let me only know your will. Amen.'

65 Sex and the Spirit

I grew up in the 1940s and 50s. In those days social values tended to reflect the values of the churches. But since then an enormous change has occurred. A yawning gap has opened up between the ethical teachings of the scriptures and those of secular society. Nowhere is this more clearly to be seen than in the inter-related areas of sexuality and marriage. Nowadays, in Christian Ireland, premarital sex is common, many couples live together without getting married, others engage in extramarital affairs, and if they separate from their spouses they find new partners. There has also been a huge increase in the availability and use of pornography. It has also been revealed that some clerics have failed to keep their vows of celibacy and have engaged in illicit and even criminal behaviours.

St Paul was familiar with this kind of conflict between scriptural and social ethics. The culture in which he lived was largely pagan. Its citizens hadn't experienced new life in Christ. TV host, Gerry Springer, would have felt at home with them as far as their sexual misconduct was concerned. Paul says that: 'God gave them up in the lusts of their hearts to impurity, to the degrading of their bodies among themselves ... for this reason God gave them up to degrading passions. Their women exchanged natural intercourse for unnatural, and in the same way also the men, giving up natural intercourse with women, were consumed with passion for one another' (Rom 1:24-27). In another place St Paul added: 'The works of the flesh are obvious: fornication, impurity and licentiousness' (Gal 5:19). Then he warned in an ominous way, 'Those who do such things will not inherit the kingdom of God' (Gal 5:21).

Following his conversion to Christ, St Paul came to realise that he was a new creation (2 Cor 5:17). He testified: 'Those who belong to Christ Jesus have crucified the flesh with its passions and desires' (Gal 5:24). Not only did he experience right desires where sexual morality was concerned, he had a new found ability to carry them out. Whereas in the past he could say: 'I can will what is right, but I cannot do it' (Rom 7:18), now he could say, 'I can do all things through him who strengthens me' (Phil 4:13). That is why he declared to his fellow believers: 'The spirit you received is … a spirit of power and love and self-discipline' (2 Tim 1:7). 'This is the will of God,' he declared, 'your sanctific-ation: that you abstain from fornication; that each of you know how to control your own body in holiness and honour, not with lustful passions like the Gentiles who do not know God' (1 Thess 4:3-5).

Jesus once observed, 'By their fruits you shall know them' (Mt 7:16). Judging by the widespread sexual permissiveness evident in Ireland today, there are many baptised pagans who still don't really know God. In this context the church has a solemn duty to work tirelessly to evangelise our people. It will have to do this in the firm belief that, if they form a deep personal relationship with Christ, they will have both the desire and the power to carry the yoke of Christian sexual morality. As Paul urged: 'Live by the Spirit, I say, and do not gratify the desires of the flesh. For what the flesh desires is opposed to the Spirit, and what the Spirit desires is opposed to the flesh, for they are opposed to each other' (Gal 5:16-17). Paradoxically, rather than being an unhealthy form of sexual repression, this is the only reliable path to genuine Christian freedom and wholeness.

66 Prophecy Today

The word 'prophet' is derived from the Greek *prophetes*, meaning 'spokesperson.' In other words a prophet or prophetess is someone who, under the inspiration of the Holy Spirit, speaks in a revelatory way on God's behalf. St Thomas Aquinas said that prophecy is primarily a 'divine revelation, announcing future events with unshakeable truth'. However, modern scripture scholars say that prophecy is more a matter of 'forth-telling' than 'fore-telling'. In other words, the prophet or prophetess evaluates the signs of the times in terms of the mind and heart of God. They gain this insight as a result of an inspired vision, dream or inner inspiration. Although genuine prophecy is revelatory, it merely elucidates the implications of scriptural revelation, without adding to it.

Rather than being a sign of the holiness of the prophet or prophetess, the gift of prophecy is freely granted in order to help others to grow in holiness. As Paul says in 1 Cor 14:3: 'Everyone who prophesies speaks to men for their edification, exhortation and comfort.' There are a number of ways in which prophecy does this.

Firstly, it can take the form of a message which is spontaneously inspired by the Holy Spirit and spoken into a particular situation. For example, there was a frequently quoted utterance of Bruce Yocum's in St Peter's Basilica on Easter Monday 1975 about the approaching age of darkness that was about to come upon the church and the world. Secondly, prophecy can take the form of inspired and inspiring preaching or teaching based on a scripture text. I can recall a memorable talk given by Protestant writer, David Pawson, entitled, 'It is not fair.' It was about the parable of the labourers in the vineyard in Mt 20:1-16, and was prophetic in its impact upon me. Thirdly, prophecy can take the form of a challenging public pronouncement on a moral or ethical issue that confronts current social values. I felt that part of John Paul II's address in Limerick, in 1979, about the dangers of materialism and the coming time of testing in Ireland, was prophetic in this sense.

St Paul esteemed the gift of prophecy very highly. He ranked it second after apostleship (Eph 4:11). He wished that everyone could prophecy (1 Cor 14:39). As a result he exhorted the believers to desire this gift. 'Follow the way of love,' he wrote, 'and eagerly desire spiritual gifts, especially the gift of prophecy' (1 Cor 14:1). If God answers our prayers and speaks a word of revelation though a member of the Christian community, we need to respond to it in an obedient way. As Jesus said: 'Blessed are those who hear the word of God and keep it' (Lk 11:28). Otherwise, when finally we go before God's judgement seat, we will say: 'Lord, Lord, did we not prophesy in your name' and God will reply: 'I never knew you. Away from me, you evil-doers!' (Mt 7:22-23).

Clearly, the gift of prophecy was highly esteemed in the early church. A question arises. Who are the prophets today, who are the men and women who convey God's challenging word and will to us? Why not spend some time reflecting on your answer? Try to nominate a bishop, priest, religious and lay person who, in the present time of crisis, is revealing something of God's purposes to us? Has the Christian community accepted what this person has said? (cf Mt 13:57), or would you be inclined to say with the psalmist, 'We see no signs, no prophet anymore, and none of us knows how long it will last' (Ps 74:9).

67 Why Go to Confession?

Capitalism has had a profound effect on society. From a Christian point of view, it has led, among other things, to an increase in individualism and a privatisation of religion. As a result, many Catholics have begun to loose sight of the radically communitarian dimension of the Christian life. One area where this is pretty obvious is in the traditional practice of going to the sacrament of reconciliation. Many people say, 'Why should I confess my sins to a priest when I can tell them directly to God and receive forgiveness?' It is true that God does forgives us when we ACT, by Admitting our faults, Confessing them honestly, and Trusting in divine mercy. But that is not the full picture. It bypasses the role of the community.

It is the community which enables us to sense God's mysterious presence in so many ways, for instance, by means of its caring, and religious rituals. It is the same community that we wound by our sins, pre-eminently by our lack of love. Even, if we commit secret, private sins, they reinforce our selfishness thereby making us more self-absorbed in our subsequent dealings with others. It is only right and fitting, therefore, that the community should sacramentally mediate the forgiveness of our sins on God's behalf.

It would seem that this latter point is firmly rooted in the scriptures. In Mt 18:15-18, Jesus spoke to the apostles about how to handle offences that were committed against the community. Step one. Go privately to the person and point out the fault. Step two. If you are not listened to, take one or two others along with you so that they can confirm your complaint. Step three. If that doesn't succeed, inform the church about the issue. Then Jesus adds: 'Truly I tell you, whatever you bind on earth will be bound in heaven, and whatever you loose on earth will be loosed in heaven.'

This teaching may have informed James's words: 'Confess your sins to one another, and pray for one another, that you may be healed. The fervent prayer of a righteous person is very powerful' (Jas 5:16). Instead of referring to sacramental confession this verse seemed to describe the benefits of the public admission of shortcomings with a view to having the community pray for one's forgiveness and healing. This practice was given a sacramental focus when Jesus appeared to Peter and the apostles after his resurrection. Having greeted them: 'He breathed on them and said to them, "Receive the Holy Spirit. If you forgive the sins of any, they are forgiven them; if you retain the sins of any, they are retained"' (Jn 20:22-23).

It is an ironic fact that while Catholics have been abandoning the practice of private confession, Alcoholics Anonymous has been rediscovering it. Number five of the famous twelve steps states that an admission of wrongdoing to oneself, to God and another human being, is vital for true sobriety. Addiction and its attendant evils is merely the presenting problem. It is rooted in inner hurts, low self-esteem, and shame. Addicts hate themselves for what they did and failed to do. However, if they confess the whole truth to an understanding, non-judgemental member of the community, they begin to experience self-acceptance and inner healing. They learn to love themselves as they are, and not as they could be. It seems to me that AA has rediscovered some of the wisdom that lies behind the church's belief in confession. The sacrament mediates mercy and inner healing to the individual, as a member of the Christian community.

68 Depression in the Bible

Depression is the most common emotional illness in the Western world. About one in ten of us can expect to experience it at some point in our lives. It is a feeling of sadness, loneliness, dejection, helplessness and hopelessness. It can be differentiated from normal grief, which is a state of sadness proportionate to an actual loss.

Reactive depression is the kind that is triggered by some significant loss or trauma, such as the death of a loved one. Seasonal Affective Disorder is a type of depression that tends to take hold at certain times of the year when there is a lack of sunlight. Endogenous depression, is caused by electrochemical imbalances in the brain. Manic depression, or bipolar disorder, afflicts about one per cent of the population. They tend to experience emotional extremes ranging from elation to depression. A felt sense of God's presence is often eclipsed during times of depression.

While reading the bible it has often occurred to me that it was referring to one or other of these forms of depression. In one place the writer says: 'Vanity of vanities ... All things are vanity! What profit has man from all the labour which he toils at under the sun? One generation passes and another comes, but the world forever stays.' A little later he adds: 'Nothing is new under the sun. Even the thing of which we say, "See, this is new!" has already existed in the ages that preceded us. There is no remembrance of the men of old; nor of those to come will there be any remembrance among those who come after them' (Eccl 1:2-11). If a psychiatrist heard one of his patients express apathetic and hopeless sentiments like these, he would suspect that s/he was suffering from clinical depression.

There is an example of this kind of *ennui* in the Book of Kings. Firstly we are told about Elijah's titanic struggle with the prophets of Baal. But then we are informed that his time of triumphant elation was quickly succeeded by a period of suicidal depression. We are told in symbolic words that: 'Elijah was afraid and fled for his life, going to Beer-sheba of Judah. He left his servant there and went a day's journey into the desert, until he came to a broom tree and sat beneath it. He prayed for death: 'This is enough, O Lord! Take my life, for I am no better than my fathers' (1 Kgs 19:3-5). From the sound of it, the prophet may have been suffering from severe burnout. Notice how his euphoria was followed by fear, loneliness, guilt, worthlessness, failure and a longing for death.

However, it is instructive to discover that his sense of breakdown gradually led to a spiritual breakthrough. As Ps 23:4 testifies: 'Even if I walk in the valley of darkness, I fear no evil for you are there.' Truly, the longest journey is the journey inwards. When Elijah experienced emotional exhaustion he went on to encounter his deeper self. The God within spoke to him, firstly, in a dream, i.e. the dark speech of the spirit. When, in faith, he followed the guidance he had received, it led him to have a profound religious experience. On this occasion it was not in extroverted drama, as heretofore, but in introverted silence (cf 1 Kgs 19:12). There, Elijah encountered God, and his depression lifted. With the psalmist he could testify: 'If I say, "surely the darkness shall cover me, and the light around me become night," even the darkness is not dark to you, the night is bright as day, for darkness is as light to you' (Ps 139:11-12).

69 Mary and Martha

Most of us are familiar with the story, in Lk 10:38-42, about the visit of Jesus to the home of Mary and Martha, the sisters of Lazarus. All sorts of symbolic meanings have been read into the text.

1. Some say it is about the superiority of contemplation, represented by the listening Mary, to the active life, represented by the busy Martha.

2. Others say it is about women's roles, showing that to be a disciple and prospective witness of Jesus, like Mary, is better than being a homemaker and hostess, like Martha.

3. It could be argued that this passage underlines the importance of the golden rule, of doing to others what you would want them to do you (cf Mt 7:12). Both Mary and Martha have the best of intentions. But Martha focuses on her own need to provide lavish hospitality, whereas Mary focuses on Jesus' need for an oasis of quietness and intimacy in the midst of his busy and demanding public ministry. Unlike Martha, Mary adds empathic understanding to her benevolence.

4. It has been suggested that this passage is about the primacy of priorities over needs. Love can be seen either as relationship or service. Relationship, represented by Mary, is the priority. It is more important than the need for service, represented by Martha. The latter should be the expression of relationship rather than being a substitute for it.

There is validity in each of these interpretations. However, this reflection focuses on another point.

Luke tells us that when Jesus responded to Martha's complaints about her inactive sister, he said: 'Martha, Martha, you are worried and distracted by many things, there is need for only one thing, Mary has chosen the better part, which will not be taken away from her' (Lk 10:41-42). Surely, what Jesus was highlighting was the fact that, in spite of repeatedly telling people not to fret over material things, Martha was 'worried and distracted' by a number of them. Surely, this is the real point of the story. Jesus is discerning that, although Martha loves him, she is being motivated, to a greater or lesser extent, by fears to do with her role. As Paul was to say sometime later: 'God did not give us a spirit of fear' (2 Tim 1:7). In other words, her fear comes from her ego and its concerns, rather than from God and the inspirations of divine grace.

In this regard one is reminded of what Jesus said to the disciples on another occasion: 'Do not worry; do not say, "What are we to eat? What are we to drink?" ... It is the gentiles who set their hearts on all these things. Your heavenly Father knows you need them all. Set your hearts on his kingdom first, and on God's saving justice, and all these other things will be given you as well' (Mt 6:31-34). In other words, focus on God and on God's purposes, as they are revealed in and through Jesus, rather than on your own agenda, no matter how well intentioned it is. Mary is an example of this kind of single-minded attention.

When you do this, you will no longer be motivated by performance anxiety, as Martha was. As St John was to comment years later: 'There is no fear in love, but perfect love (like Mary's) casts out fear; for fear (like Martha's) has to do with punishment (i.e. of being condemned for falling short of what is expected)' (1 Jn 4:18). Ideally, there should be no conflict in this story. The contemplation typified by Mary should be expressed in the practical action which is typified by Martha.

70 Asking For a Sign

Many years ago, I heard a woman say, 'I'm going to cast a fleece before the Lord.' I had no idea what she meant. It was only afterwards that I discovered that her comment was derived from a passage in Judges 6:36-40. Gideon was a hero-liberator of his people. On one occasion he felt called to lead his clan against the Midianites and their chiefs. Gideon experienced doubts about his prospective task. Was he really called by God to engage in this demanding and dangerous military campaign?

Gideon decided he would ask the Lord for a sign, one that would confirm whether God would be on his side during the impending battle. So he said: 'I am going to lay a fleece of wool on the threshing floor; if there is dew on the fleece alone, and it is dry on all the ground, then I shall know that you will deliver Israel by my hand, as you have said.' When Gideon got up in the morning his fleece was damp. This was no miracle, however. For many years, men living in one of the arid desert areas of Israel had obtained enough water to sustain them by spreading out fleeces in the evening. The following morning they would wring out the dew from them.

Not fully satisfied by the first sign, Gideon asked for a second; this time a miraculous one. 'Let me,' he said to the Lord, 'make trial with the fleece just once more; let it be dry on the fleece, and on the ground let there be due.' We are informed that God answered his request. The ground was damp and the fleece was dry. So when the woman said she would cast a fleece before the Lord, it was a biblical way of saying that she was going to ask God for a sign to confirm whether something she intended doing was in accord with the divine will or not.

A question. Is it a good thing to ask God for a sign? Normally no. God wants us to establish whether our promptings come from the Lord or not by means of discernment of spirits. If they are associated, inwardly, with on-going consolation of spirit such as peace, joy and hope, they are probably from God. If they are associated with desolation of spirit, such as agitation, restlessness, and anxiety, they are probably not from God. For example, when John XXIII became Pope he had a desire to convene an ecumenical council. He sought the help of a competent spiritual director. Together they engaged in discernment of spirits. Happily, Pope John came to see that his urge to initiate the Second Vatican Council had been prompted by the Holy Spirit, rather than his human spirit, or the evil spirit.

That said, spiritual directors maintain that if people are in a state of on-going desolation of spirit, they cannot engage in the form of discernment already mentioned. In situations like this they might ask for some kind of confirmatory sign. For example, many years ago I received what I thought was a private revelation. It contained the words, 'rebuild the walls of Jerusalem.' As I was in a state of desolation, I couldn't engage in discernment of spirits. I asked God to confirm whether the revelation was inspired by the Holy Spirit. With my eyes shut, I would open the bible at random. If my finger was on the words, 'rebuild the walls of Jerusalem' I would believe my message came from God. When I opened the bible my finger was on Ps 51:18 which says: 'rebuild the walls of Jerusalem!'

71 Impossible Odds

Recently, on an underground train, I heard one woman tell her friend how she had applied for a government job. Apparently, there were a large number of applicants, but they were whittled down on the basis of their qualifications, interviews, and other tests. In the book of Judges we are told that God wanted an army to be assembled in order to attack the Midianites. Thirty two thousand men enlisted. The Lord thought it was too many. If such a sizeable army was victorious, it would claim the credit for itself. So God drastically reduced the numbers by inspiring Gideon, the commander in chief, to quote Deut 20:8 which says: 'Is anyone afraid or disheartened? He should go back to his house, or he might cause the heart of his comrades to melt like his own.' When the men heard these words, as many as 20,000 of them returned home. God still thought there were too many. Another test was needed.

Gideon was instructed to watch how his soldiers drank when they reached a river. 'All those who lap the water with their tongues, as a dog laps, you shall put to one side, all those who kneel down to drink, putting their hands to their mouths, you shall put to one side.' When Gideon did this there were only 300 men who had lapped the water. Then the Lord told him to dismiss the others. Why did the Lord want the men who had lapped the water to remain? Robert Bowling suggests in his authoritative Anchor Bible commentary on Judges, that those who scooped up the water with their hands showed themselves to be more watchful and ready to meet any sudden emergency, such as an attack from the rear. Strangely, it was not those men the Lord chose, but rather the less alert ones who lay on the ground and lapped the water. It was if God was saying that victory would come, 'not by might, nor by power, but by my Spirit, says the Lord of hosts' (Zech 4:6). In the event, Gideon and his small band of men, defeated the Midianites.

It would seem that there are at least two important, but inter-related, lessons to be gleaned from this story. Firstly, if the Lord chooses a person, or a group to do some task, they shouldn't be surprised if they are not the most talented and experienced people available. Remember what St Paul said in 1 Cor 1:16-31: 'Consider your own call, brothers and sisters; not many of you were wise by human standards, not many were powerful, not many were of noble birth. But God chose what is foolish in the world to shame the strong ... so that no one might boast in the presence of the Lord.'

Secondly, even if the task seems impossible from a human point of view, due to a lack of numbers and material resources, it will become possible if it is an expression of God's will. Those involved can be sure of divine help. So they can pray with assurance: 'Yahweh, no one but you can stand up for the powerless against the powerful. Come to our help. Yahweh our God! We rely on you, and confront this challenge in your name. Yahweh, you are our God. We leave everything to you' (2 Chron 14:11). What the Lord repeatedly said before impending battles can be extended to all the challenging situations we have to face: 'Do not be afraid! Stand by and see the salvation of the Lord which he will accomplish for you today ... The Lord will fight for you while you keep silent' (Ex 14:13).

72 Grieving the Spirit

In Eph 4:30 we read: 'Do not grieve the Spirit of God, with which you were marked with a seal for the day of redemption.' Let's begin with the notion of being sealed with the Spirit. When we receive baptism and confirmation we are sealed with the imprint of God's grace. This notion was derived from the practice of putting a seal of hot wax on official documents. Then a signet ring was pressed into the soft wax. The resulting image was a pledge of the solemn undertakings they often contained. Likewise, the imprint of God's Spirit, is a pledge that those who bear the divine likeness within, will belong to Jesus until he comes again.

When we consciously appropriate the graces we received in the sacraments of initiation, we are enabled to grasp the length and breadth, the height and depth of God's unconditional love for us. At the same time we experience a desire to express that same love to everyone we meet.

People who live by the Spirit do not satisfy the selfish desires of the flesh (cf Gal 5:16). The Spirit gives them both the desire and the power to relate and to act in a loving way. As Paul says: 'Owe no one anything, except to love one another, for the one who loves another has fulfilled the law' (Rom 13:8). In another place he described the qualities of that love. It is patient and kind, it is not envious, boastful, arrogant or rude. It doesn't insist on its own way; it is not irritable, resentful or happy about wrongdoing, but rejoices in the truth. It bears, believes, hopes and endures all things (cf 1 Cor 13:4-8).

Eph 4:30 also says, 'Don't grieve the Spirit of God.' This notion is derived from a text in Is 63:10 which tells us that the people of the time: 'Rebelled and grieved God's Holy Spirit.' The notion of rebellion implies a willful rejection of the ordinances of the Lord. So it is with Christians who are lured, by the world, the flesh, and the devil; they override the loving impulses that the Spirit prompts within them. Every time they do so, the Holy Spirit is saddened. It is progressively quenched, like a candle flame being deprived of oxygen. As a result such people are less aware of the divine indwelling and the loving inclinations that God tries to prompt within them.

I have also noticed that when believers grieve God's Holy Spirit, consolation gives way to desolation of spirit. It is an emotional feeling of God's absence. Spiritual things like prayer, scripture reading and the sacraments are less attractive. Instead, there is a worldly preoccupation with base things like pleasure, power and popularity.

Rather than seeing sin in impersonal and legalistic terms, as a failure to keep God's laws, mature Christians see it as a willful failure to receive and express the love of God in a single-minded, credible way. This not only grieves the Holy Spirit within them, it also grieves their own spirits which are closely united to Christ by the same Spirit. Hopefully, as Paul said: 'Godly grief leads to a repentance that leads to salvation and brings no regret' (2 Cor 7:10). In other words, having become aware of tears of sadness flowing down the cheeks of their grieving Lord, they themselves weep with sorrow as they acknowledge how they have failed to walk by the Holy Spirit (cf Gal 5:16). But as Jesus promised in the Beatitudes: 'Blessed are those who mourn, for they will be comforted' (Mt 5:4), i.e. by the Holy Spirit, the Paraclete.

73 It's not fair

Christians are quite familiar with the fact that we are saved solely by means of the grace of God through our faith in Jesus Christ and not because of any merits or good works of our own. It has often occurred to me that this doctrine, which was so clearly preached by St Paul in his epistles, was implicit in a number of the parables of Jesus.

For example, in the story of the labourers in the vineyard (Mt 20:1-16), we are told how men who were hired at different times, some early in the day, others at a later hour, were all paid the same wage. Those who worked the longest and the hardest received the one denarius they had been promised. But those who had worked for only a short time were also paid a denarius. Not surprisingly, the early-comers felt that their employer hadn't been fair when latecomers were paid same amount they themselves had received.

In the parable the early-comers represent the Jewish leaders of Jesus' day who tended to believe that salvation was a matter of merit rather than mercy. A person would get what s/he deserved from God as a result of his or her good works. Remember how the Pharisee in the synagogue boasted of his good works when he said: 'God, I thank you that I am not like other men, robbers, evildoers, adulterers, or even like this tax collector. I fast twice a week and give a tenth of all I get' (Lk 18:11-12).

Many years ago, a girl of seventeen went to a prayer meeting in Northern Ireland. She was a fairly typical teenager, more interested in boys and fashion than in God and religion. Nevertheless, she was deeply touched by the Lord during the meeting and received an outpouring of the Holy Spirit. A few days later I met an elderly nun who had attended the same meeting. She said to me with a pained expression: 'Fr, I have been in religious life for over forty years. I have kept the vows of poverty, chastity and obedience, prayed every day, received the sacraments, and served the poor. But I have never received an outpouring of the Holy Spirit. Then, last week, a frivolous young girl came casually to the meeting and she was richly blessed by God. It's just not fair!' Clearly, she envied the teenager's good fortune. In doing so, she was identifying with the complaint of the early comers in the parable.

Envy of this kind resents the unmerited generosity of God to others. In other words, envy is ultimately a self-centred feeling of antagonism to the whole notion of grace. The afflicted person does not want to depend on God for his or her blessings. S/he wants to deserve them. That is why invidious comparisons are made with others. 'Am I going to be outdone by his or her merits?' No wonder envious people resent the undeserved blessings others receive, whether of nature or grace. In terms of strict justice they not only consider them as being grossly unfair, they also find that they profoundly threaten their individualistic sense of significance as self-reliant men and women.

We need to have a grateful sense that all gifts, our own and those of others, are unmerited. As Jesus asked: 'Why be envious because God is generous?' (Mt 20:15). St John Chrysostom once wisely wrote: 'Would you like to see God glorified by you? Then rejoice in your brother or sister's progress and you will immediately give glory to God. Because his servant could conquer envy by rejoicing in the merits of others.'

74 The Great Command

Jesus described the essence of Christian ethics when he said: 'Love the Lord your God with all your heart and with all your soul and with all your mind. This is the first and greatest commandment. And the second is like it: Love your neighbour as yourself. All the Law and the Prophets hang on these two commandments' (Mt 22:37-40).

When I was a young man I found the first half of this precept hard to understand. How can one love a mysterious God who is beyond the grasp of the senses, or the comprehension of the imaginative or rational mind. I used to think that love for God was synonymous with love of the neighbour. To love the neighbour we could see was tantamount to loving the God we couldn't see (cf 1 Jn 4:20). While it is true that both forms of love are interrelated, they are distinct. Over the years, I have come to see that the love of the neighbour is subordinate to the love of God. It should be the expression of that love rather than being a substitute for it, as it often is in our secularised culture.

How do we love God with our whole selves? We do so when we come to appreciate who God is and what God is like. This is the result of a threefold process. Firstly, we need to have a wholehearted desire to know the Lord. Secondly, we need to pay self-forgetful and sustained attention to the twin bibles of creation and the scriptures, in the belief that they can and do mediate the presence of God. Thirdly, we need to be receptive to divine revelation, intimations of the Beyond who is in the midst of everyday life. As we do this, we can come to perceive something of the glory, greatness, goodness, graciousness, and generosity of the God who is the giver of endless gifts of grace. As we approve of these qualities and attributes we are led to spontaneously thank and praise God. In doing so, we are loving the Lord. I say this because the word 'thank' in English literally means 'to be mindful,' and the word 'praise' means to 'know the price or value' of something. So when we worship God we are calling to mind God's worth. It is fascinating to discover that the word 'love' in English is derived from the old high-German, *gilob* which means 'precious'. It in turn is derived from *lob* which means 'praise'. So when we come to appreciate something of God's worth by means of prayerful contemplation and subsequently express our approval in the form of sincere adoration, we are loving God.

We also show our love for God by escaping from the gravitational pull of self-absorption, which focuses on how God can satisfy our personal needs, by focusing on how we might respond to God's needs. At that particular point of growth, we might say from our hearts: 'Your will be done on earth as it is in heaven' (Mt 6:10). We utter this prayer, not as a matter of cheerless, legal obligation, but rather as a matter of enthusiastic, personal conviction. What we discover is that God wants two interrelated things. Firstly, the Lord desires us to experience something of the ineffable length and breadth, height and depth of Christ's unconditional love for us (Eph 3:18). Secondly, the Lord wants us to show that same love, in an unrestricted way, to the people we meet, especially the poor and needy (Jn 13:34). By doing this in everyday life, we are expressing our love for God.

75 Interpreting Scripture

With the Spirit's help, Christians have to learn to interpret the authentic meaning of the scriptures in a non-fundamentalist way. The saints had a good deal of valuable guidance to offer in this regard. St Bede wrote in the eighth century: 'The sacred scriptures are interpreted in a fourfold way. In all holy books one should ascertain what deeds are recalled and what everlasting truths are intimated in the text, what commands or counsels are there contained, and what future events are foretold.' Let's take a closer look at each of St Bede's recommendations by focusing, by way of example, on references to the temple in Jerusalem.

When he says that we should try to ascertain what deeds are recalled, he is referring to the literal meaning of the scriptures. It is discovered by painstaking research which seeks to discover such things as the historical background and the meanings intended by the authors of the different biblical books. For example, if the Jerusalem temple is mentioned, we can rely on archeological findings to augment what we know about it during the lifetime of Jesus. The other three forms of interpretation seek to establish the spiritual meaning of the scriptures, those intended by the individual authors, and those implicit in the texts.

Firstly, there is the metaphorical meaning of scripture texts. Frequently an object or event represents everlasting truths which are indirectly intimated in the text. For example, mention of the temple in Jerusalem could be interpreted as a symbolic reference to the church, the people of God. When he addressed the Christian community in 1 Cor 3:16-17 Paul said: 'Don't you know that you yourselves are God's temple and that God's Spirit lives in you? If anyone destroys God's temple, God will destroy him; for God's temple is sacred, and you are that temple.' There is undoubted merit in this form of metaphorical interpretation. But I must confess, if it losses touch with the literal meaning of the text, as it did in some of the writings of the Fathers of the Church, I find it far fetched and arbitrary.

Secondly, St Bede refers to the commands or counsels that

are contained in the scriptures. They are intended to lead us to act appropriately as Christians. St Paul had this in mind when he said that the scriptures were written 'for our instruction' (cf 2 Tim 3:16). If the temple in Jerusalem was to be interpreted in this moral sense, it could be seen as a symbol of the human body and its various experiences. Speaking about this, St Paul says: 'Flee from sexual immorality. All other sins a man commits are outside his body, but he who sins sexually sins against his own body. Do you not know that your body is a temple of the Holy Spirit' (1 Cor 6:18-19).

Thirdly, St Bede refers to the fact that sometimes scripture texts are about future events and heavenly things. When Christians appreciate the deeper spiritual meaning of a text, it can contain intimations of transcendental and eternal realities. For instance when Jesus predicted the destruction of the temple in Jerusalem (Mt 24:1-2), it was also a symbolic image of the end times. In Rev 11:19 the temple becomes a symbol of God's eternal dwelling: 'Then God's temple in heaven was opened, and within his temple was seen the ark of his covenant.'

You may be interested to know that in April 1993, The Pontifical Biblical Commission published *The Interpretation of the Bible in the Church* which was written by Cardinal Ratzinger and introduced by Pope John Paul II. Be advised. It is a rather scholarly document.

76 God and Religion

When Job was enduring great suffering, three of his friends came to visit him. They sat observing him, silently, for a long time. They were aware of his afflictions, but failed to pay attention in an empathic way. Theirs was a more insouciant, apathetic and objective form of relationship. The three of them sensed that if they attended, in an open-minded way, to Job's sufferings and their implications, they would have to face a religious dilemma. They'd have to let go of their current understanding of good and evil, without necessarily being able to replace it with a new one. In the event they were more concerned with theological orthodoxy, and the sense of personal security it gave them, than they were with the disquieting challenge posed by Job's situation. Clearly they trusted more in the religion of God than they did in the God of religion. They argued that, although Job seemed to be a good man, he must have offended God is some secret way. How else could his plight be explained? So in the name of a religious truth, they denied the truth of Job's lived experience.

Some contemporary Christians seem to do much the same. They appear to rely on the externals of religion, rather than God, for their sense of security. As a result they can feel threatened in may ways, for instance, when trusted bishops and priests are shown to have had feet of clay; when some of their cherished beliefs, such as a naïve interpretation of the creation story, are called into question; and when upsetting changes in liturgy and church structures are recommended by the Pope and bishops. Although those who are very opposed to such changes may proffer all kinds of impressive arguments in support of their case, I suspect that rather than clinging to God, they cling in a rather idolatrous way to the trappings of religion for security. They are like children who cling to security blankets and other objects, as substitutes for dependence on their mothers. Analogously, some contemporary Christians seem to cling to the externals of religion as a substitute for dependence on the Lord of religion.

Recently I came across an instructive example of true religious trust. When Catholics were in mortal danger during the English Reformation, St Thomas More's daughter, Margaret, asked her father if he was going follow the example of bishop John Fisher. He replied: 'Verily, daughter, I never intend (God being my good Lord) to pin my soul to another man's back, not even the best man that I know this day living. For I know not whether he may able to carry it. There is no man living, of whom while he lives, I may make myself sure.' Notice how St Thomas was relying on God, not on a mere man, even though John Fisher would be canonised some years later. He would have heartily endorsed the psalmist's words: 'The Lord is my rock, my fortress and my deliverer; my God is my rock, in whom I take refuge' (Ps 18:2).

Those who trust in God alone are truly secure. The edifice of their faith is built upon that firm rock. When the day of adversity comes, as it has done in recent years in the Catholic Church, they can stand firm. When the rain comes down, the streams rise, and the winds blow and beat against the house of their Christian life, it does not fall, because it has its foundation on the rock (cf Mt 7:25). As for those whose faith rests on the sands of religiosity, they are often swept away when the day of disillusionment comes.

77 Do What You Can

At times God's will is very demanding. Even when we want to carry it out, it often happens that we don't seem to have either the ability or resources to do so. However, the story of the multiplication of the loaves and fish in Jn 6:1-15, gives us encouragement. If we offer the Lord the bread of our good intentions and the fish of our limited resources, God will bless them and make good what is lacking. We will be given the power to do what, at first sight, seemed to be impossible from a human point of view.

When one reads the lives of saintly men and women who have accomplished great things for God, one almost invariably finds that they were inspired by this kind of unwavering confidence. For example, a few years ago a Jesuit priest called Rick Thomas formed a prayer group in Juarez, New Mexico. On one occasion the members reflected on the parable of the great supper in Mt 22:1-14. When the invited guests turned down the king's request to come, the monarch invited the halt, the lame and the blind to attend. As a result of prayerful reflection and discussion on this text, the prayer group members felt that the Lord wanted them to do something similar by feeding the poor.

Their first initiative involved a visit to the local rubbish dump where a number of poor people lived. They made a meagre living by scavenging. The prayer group brought food and drink to feed the number they thought they would meet. In the event there were many more than they expected. Although they didn't want to disappoint anyone, they knew that their desires exceeded their ability. Fr Rick encouraged them to trust in the One who feeds the birds of the air and the lilies of the field (cf Mt 6:26-28). The people stepped out in faith, distributed what they had, and found that, inexplicably, they had more than enough to go round.

Some time later, on Christmas day, the same group were led to bring food and drink to the prisoners in the local jail. They prepared home-made lemonade and tortillas for about a hundred inmates. However, when they arrived at the prison, they discovered that there were over two hundred prisoners expecting to be fed. When the lay-people pointed this out to Fr Rick, he reminded them of what had happened at the rubbish dump some months before and said: 'We are trying to do God's will, give out what we have, and leave the rest to God.' So they distributed their limited supply of food and drink. It never ran out. Fr Rick and his companions still believe that it multiplied in a miraculous way.

When the Rev Cecil Kerr of the Christian Renewal Centre in Rostrevor, County Down, and Sister Consilio Fitzgerald of the Cuan Mhuire rehabilitation centres were embarking on their respective projects, they too had to rely on the providence and provision of the Lord. This sense of absolute dependence gave them the assurance that God would supply whatever was lacking. As each of them dedicated themselves to following God's will in a spirit of trust, the money and materials they needed simply came their way through the spontaneous generosity of others, sometimes in remarkable ways.

I suspect that the reason why saintly Christian leaders achieve so much is the fact that they have a God-given ability to think big and to embark on great projects. They can do this because they know that God is at work within them both to will and to accomplish the divine purposes (cf Phil 2:13).

78 Power to Change

When I was studying in the US, many years ago, I ended up smoking about thirty cigarettes a day. At the time I was living on the third floor of a large hospital in Boston. To get to my room, I had to pass through the chest ward. Every time I did so, I heard patients wheezing, coughing and gasping for breath. Many of them had been heavy smokers. I thought to myself, 'If I don't give up smoking I could end up suffering from bronchitis, emphysema or lung cancer.' I was convinced that God wouldn't want me to risk the gift of my health in this way. So, I had a growing desire to kick the habit.

There was a problem. I had often tried to stop smoking in the past, but without success. There had been one humiliating experience of defeat after another. In the words of St Paul, 'I decided to do good, but I didn't really do it; I decided not to do bad, but then I did it anyway. My decisions, such as they were, didn't result in actions ... It happened so regularly that it was predictable' (Rom 7:19-20). I think that anyone who is enslaved either by an addiction or a sinful habit could identify with these words. We can have the desire to change, but not the power to do so. As St Paul said: 'I tried everything and nothing helped. I was at the end of my rope. Was there no one who could do anything for me? Wasn't that the real question?' (Rom 7:24).

Happily, St Paul went on to provide a response. 'The answer thank God, is that Jesus Christ can and does. He acted to set things right in this life of contradictions where I wanted to serve God with all my heart and mind, but was pulled by the influence of sin to do something totally different' (Rom 7:25). In general terms, Alcoholics Anonymous and all other twelve-step programmes, would agree with what Paul had to say. Only personal relationship with God and utter reliance on the Lord's power can enable us to change. That is why steps two and three of AA declare: 'We came to believe in a power greater than ourselves could restore us to sanity. So we made a decision to turn our will and our lives over to the care of God as we understood him.'

At the age of 29 I had offered my life to the Lord. I experienced such an outpouring of the Holy Spirit that my awareness of God began to change. In the words of Paul: 'I lived by faith in the Son of God who loved me and gave his life for me' (Gal 2:20). In Boston, I can remember handing my will over to him and saying, 'Lord, I want to do your will by giving up smoking, but I will only be able to do so by the power of your Holy Spirit at work within me.' That was in 1983. By the grace of God I have never smoked a cigarette since then. I had discovered the power to change.

If you have a desire to know God or to give up an addiction or sinful habit, know that the power to change is available. It is the Holy Spirit, whose divine 'power is made perfect in our weakness' (2 Cor 12:9). So ask the Spirit of God to overshadow you, as it did the apostles and disciples at Pentecost. Then you will experience the transformation for yourself. You will also know that the same power could transform our families, communities and nation.

79 Courageous Perseverance

The notion of perseverance has always attracted me. It is the ability to stick to and complete the undertakings and solemn commitments we have made, no matter what the cost. Not surprisingly, it is spoken about in the New Testament. The Greek word for perseverance means 'to remain in place, to stand firm, to endure, to stand by someone, or to remain in an occupation or state.'

Jesus practised this kind of courageous perseverance in his life, especially during his temptations in the wilderness and again during Passion Week. In the Garden of Gethsemane the prospect of his impending agony was daunting in the extreme. In the words of Heb 5:7, 'he offered up prayers and supplications with loud cries and tears to him who was able to save him from death.' But as Matthew attests, Jesus prayed: 'Father, if it be possible, let this cup pass from me; nevertheless, not as I will, but as you will' (Mt 26:39). When it became apparent that the Father wanted him to endure suffering and death, Jesus persevered with courage to the bitter end. As scripture says we look to him as 'the pioneer and perfecter of faith, who for the joy that was set before him endured the cross, despising the shame' (Heb 12:2).

Jesus also spoke about the need for constancy and steadfastness. 'No one,' he said, 'who puts his hand to the plough and looks back is fit for the kingdom of God' (Lk 9:62). On another occasion he spoke about a father who asked his two sons to work in his vineyard. One said he wouldn't do so, but afterwards changed his mind. The other enthusiastically said yes, but in the event he didn't show up. Jesus asked, 'Which of the two did the will of the father?' and his listeners responded 'The first' (Mt 21:28-31). In other words, if you have undertaken to do something, in the belief that it is God's will for you, don't change course for any reason. With God's help stick to your commitment, for otherwise you will not be worthy of fellowship with God.

Christians are called to imitate the perseverance of Christ. Talking of the trials and tribulations that would afflict them,

Jesus said: 'You will be hated by all because of my name. But the one who perseveres to the end will be saved' (Mk 13:13). There are a number of situations where this endurance and patient perseverance is particularly needed today:

1. When we suffer physical and emotional ill health, together with misfortunes of one kind or another.

2. When we endure desolation of spirit and are buffeted by temptations because we no longer enjoy a heartfelt sense of God's presence and consolations.

3. When as a result of crises in our vocation, whether in the context of marriage, priesthood or religious life, we feel like abandoning our commitments for more attractive options.

4. When we are misunderstood, criticised and even persecuted because of our Christian beliefs and morals, we may be inclined to hide or even deny them.

If these things happen, St Paul says that we should: 'exult in our hardships, understanding that hardship develops perseverance, and perseverance develops a tested character, something that gives us hope, a hope that will not let us down' (Rom 5:3). St James added: 'You know well that the testing of your faith produces perseverance, and perseverance must complete its work so that you will become fully developed, complete, not deficient in any way' (Jas 1:3). So, pray for the grace of faithfulness that you may 'run with perseverance the race that is set before us' (Heb 12:1).

80 Forms of Christian Witness

Before his return to his Father in heaven Jesus spoke these memorable words to the apostles: 'You will receive power when the Holy Spirit has come upon you; and you will be my witnesses in Jerusalem , in all Judea and Samaria and to the ends of the earth' (Acts 1:8). Shortly after the ascension, the promised Holy Spirit was poured out on Pentecost. Immediately, the apostles entered into a new and deeply personal relationship with Jesus as the divine Son of God. He was their Saviour, who loved them unconditionally. Immediately, they not only experienced a strong desire to bear witness to this good news, they had the God-given ability to do so effectively. In Acts, St Luke described how the good news spread out in ever widening circles to the ends of the earth. Paul completed the process by bearing witness to Christ in Rome, which lay at the very heart of the known world.

Contemporary Christians are also called to bear witness to the outpouring of God's merciful love in and through Jesus Christ. Only a personal Pentecost, whether as a result of a dramatic religious awakening, or a more gradual process of blessing, can lead us into a conscious awareness of God's liberating presence and power. This is vitally important because only people who have had a personal experience, as opposed to a theoretical knowledge of the good news, can bear credible witness to God's love. There are three main ways in which this can be done. Firstly, by preaching and teaching; secondly by a life well lived, deeds of mercy and action for justice; and thirdly by charismatic deeds of power such as healings, exorcism and miracles.

Scripture underlines the importance of leading people to believe in the good news by means of inspired preaching and teaching. It says: 'How could they (the unbelievers) have faith in him (Christ) without having heard of him? And how could they hear without someone to spread the news? And how could anyone spread the news without being sent? ... So then faith comes from hearing, and hearing through the word of Christ' (Rom 10:14-17). Nowadays we need anointed homilists who only preach what God has revealed to them in prayer. We also need committed catechists and religion teachers, whether in the classroom or the home, who only impart what they themselves personally know and believe.

Verbal witness needs to find expression in a life well lived. St Peter said that a Christian wife could convert her pagan husband by deeds rather than words (cf 1 Pet 3:1) Pope Paul VI echoed this sentiment in his encyclical on evangelisation: 'Modern people,' he wrote, 'are wary of teachers but impressed by witness, and if they listen to teachers it is only because they bear witness first' (par 41). In this regard the church has always stressed the importance of corporal and spiritual works of mercy, especially generosity to the poor. It also emphasises the importance of identifying the unjust and oppressive causes of poverty and working to change them by means of appropriate political and social action.

In the lives of Jesus and the apostles, healings, exorcisms and miracles astonished and amazed unbelievers. They were the good news in action. Members of the modern Charismatic Movement maintain that some members of the church are called and gifted to bear similar witness to the good news by means of charismatic deeds of power, especially healing. Scripture supports this view. Having commissioned the apostles to witness to him, Jesus said: 'These signs will accompany those who believe … they will lay their hands on the sick and they will recover' (Mk 16:17-18).

81 Panic Attacks

There is a humorous but perceptive adage which says, 'A neurotic is someone who builds castles in the air and a psychotic is someone who lives in them.' One could say that neurotics are people who are unrealistic in one area of their lives as a result of being hijacked by material from their unconscious. Psychotics are those who are unrealistic in every area of their lives as a result of irrational feelings which swamp them from within. While most of us are neurotic to a greater or lesser extent, there may be times of breakdown when we are haunted by high anxiety. It may come as a surprise to know that even the saints had experiences like this.

For example, shortly after the death of her mother and the departure of her elder sister to the local Carmelite convent, Thérèse of Lisieux developed a mysterious illness. It started with violent headaches. She became delirious and had convulsions. Her sister Leoine says that the bouts of illness looked 'like continual attacks of delirious terror, often accompanied by convulsions. Her screeches were frightening, her eyes were full of terror and her face was contracted with pain. Nails in the wall took on terrible forms in her eyes, forms that frightened the life out of her. Often she didn't even recognise us. One evening especially she was terrified when my father approached her with his hat in his hand; to her it looked like some terrible beast.' Leonie says that the attacks ended in a miraculous way when she and her sister Marie prayed fervently to our Lady, that their sister would be cured. She was.

It is consoling to find that the bible was acquainted with this kind of high anxiety. There is a haunting passage in the Old Testament which describes how at one point during the plagues of Egypt, darkness covered the Egyptians while the Israelites still enjoyed the light. 'For fear is nothing but a giving up of the helps that come from reason; and hope, defeated by this inward weakness, prefers ignorance of what causes the torment. But throughout the night, which was really powerless and which came upon them from the recesses of powerless Hades, they all

slept the same sleep, and now were driven by monstrous spec-
tres, and now were paralysed by their souls' surrender; for sudden and unexpected fear overwhelmed them. And whoever was
there fell down, and thus was kept shut up in a prison not made
of iron' (Wis 17:12-16). The inspired writer goes on to say that
every natural sound, even the sweet melody of birds, paralysed
the Egyptians with fear.

If you are prone to bouts of high anxiety, what should you
do? Firstly, realise that your feelings, no matter how strong they
are, are not facts. You are not being drawn into a chaotic vortex
of radical insecurity. God is present and has a benevolent plan
for your life and provides for you. Secondly, the Lord says to
you, 'Do not be afraid, I am with you; do not be dismayed, I am
your God; I will strengthen you, I will help you, I will uphold
you with my victorious right hand' (Is 41:10). So St Peter advises:
'Cast your anxieties on the Lord, for he cares about you' (1 Pet
4:7). Hebrews 13:6 adds: 'We can say with confidence: The Lord
is my helper, I will not be afraid; what can man do to me?' These
promises of the Lord will be fulfilled when, with the Spirit's empowering help, you make a determined act of will, with God's
help, not to be mastered by fear.

82 Unity of Mind and Heart

There is an idealistic description of the early Christian community in Acts 4:32-36. It reads: 'Now the company of those who believed were of one heart and soul, and no one said that any of the things which he possessed was his own, but they had everything in common.' When Luke talked about unity and sharing in the early church, he was implicitly saying that it fulfilled, with the Spirit's help, the ancient Greek ideal of friendship. For instance, Pythagoras had written in the fifth century BC: 'Friends share in the perfect communion of a single spirit and have everything in common.'

Although some members of the early Christian church may have been intimate friends, I don't think that Luke was implying that all the members were necessarily sharing their innermost thoughts and feelings with one another. They were one in mind and heart in so far as they were conformed to the mind and heart of Christ. St Paul seemed to endorse this interpretation when he said in Phil 2:5: 'Be of the same mind, having the same love, being in full accord and of one mind ... Let the same mind be in you that was in Christ.' This ideal was echoed elsewhere in the New Testament. Rom 15:5-6 says: 'May the God who gives endurance and encouragement give you a spirit of unity among yourselves as you follow Christ Jesus so that with one heart and mouth you may glorify the God and Father of our Lord Jesus Christ'; and in 1 Cor 1:10 we read: 'I appeal to you, brothers and sisters, in the name of our Lord Jesus Christ, that all of you agree with one another so that there may be no divisions among you and that you may be perfectly united in mind and thought.' And 1 Pet 3:8 says: 'Finally, all of you, live in harmony with one another; be sympathetic, love as brothers and sisters, be compassionate and humble.'

These ideals were in the minds of the founders of monasticism and the religious orders that followed them. For example, for many years St Augustine lived with a group of friends including Alypius and Nebridius. They engaged in study and the mutual pursuit of wisdom. This communal lifestyle, before and after his conversion, led Augustine to write the oldest monastic rule in western Christianity. It proposed an ideal of communal friendships that would be expressed in shared property, living together in harmony, and being 'of one mind and one heart' (Rule 11).

Acts 4:33 made it clear that those who desired to be effective evangelisers needed to be members of united Christian communities. Not only would harmonious relationships inspire effective preaching and teaching, they would act as icons to the truth of their good news message. St Vincent de Paul shared this vision of community life. Speaking to some of his missionaries, who were soon to depart for Ireland in the seventeenth century, he said: 'How will we ever be able to draw souls together in Jesus Christ if you are not united among yourselves and with him? It will not be possible. Have then but one heart and one will. Otherwise you will be acting like horses who, when they are hitched to a plough, some pull in one direction others in another, and thus they spoil and ruin everything. God calls you to work in his vineyard. Go then, having one heart and intention, and by this means you will produce fruit.'

Wherever members of the contemporary church encounter mistrust, resentment and divisions, they need to work assiduously to overcome them in a spirit of unconditional love.

83 Accentuate the Positive

Some time ago, a reporter with *The Irish Examiner* interviewed me. He wanted to know if Catholics could use some of the exercises which are familiar to the practitioners of Yoga. I said they could if they didn't subscribe to the Hindu beliefs that inform them. I also referred him to par 16 of *Some Aspects of Christian Meditation*, published in Rome in 1989. It says: 'The majority of the great religions which have sought union with God in prayer have also pointed out ways to achieve it. Just as the Catholic Church rejects nothing of what is true and holy in these religions, neither should these ways be rejected out of hand simply because they are not Christian. On the contrary, one can take from them what is useful so long as the Christian conception of prayer, its logic and requirements are never obscured.'

Like many other biblical writers, St Paul had catholic tastes in the sense that they were universal. He wasn't afraid to acknowledge the truth, no matter where it found it. For example, Stoicism was a school of philosophy that had been founded in Athens in the third century BC. It was still influential in New Testament times. Indeed, a prominent Stoic, called Seneca, may have corresponded with St Paul. In Phil 4:8 the latter was probably referring to Stoic ideals when he said poetically: 'Finally beloved, whatever is true, whatever is honourable, whatever is just, whatever is pure, whatever is pleasing, whatever is commendable, if there is any excellence and if there is anything worthy of praise, think about these things and the God of peace will be with you.'

The apostle probably mentioned Stoic values, in an approving way, for two main reasons. Firstly, he had conscientious pagans, like the Stoics, in mind when he stated: 'the requirements of the law are written on their hearts, their consciences also bearing witness, and their conflicting thoughts accuse or even defend them' (Rom 2:15). In other words, God had revealed something of the moral law to non-Christians. Secondly, it may be that Paul not only admired the Stoic way of looking at life, he tried to imitate some of its ethical teachings, and invited the Phillipians to imitate his example (cf Phil 4:9).

As his many letters show, St Paul was well aware of the shortcomings of the people around him. But he seemed to be saying to the Phillipians, 'Avoid the tendency to measure everyone and against some abstract ideal of perfection, in such a way that you will inevitably find fault with them. Even if people or groups have many failings, don't focus on them. Instead, concentrate on any redeeming qualities they seem to have. When you encounter what is strange, unfamiliar and a little threatening in other religions and cultures, try also to avoid the kind of unthinking prejudice that would blind you to what is worthwhile within them. Appreciate these positive things with heartfelt gratitude and you will enjoy true peace of mind and heart.'

So we Catholics need to avoid the kind of reactionary conservatism that seems to be quite common nowadays. Its proponents cannot affirm any truths or values that are different from their own. As a result they fail to perceive much that is worthwhile in the Christian Churches, modern science, different religions, New Age spirituality, the writings of agnostics and atheists etc. In Phillipians 4:8 Paul seems to be urging us to be open to what is admirable no matter where we find it. As St Thomas Aquinas once observed: 'Whatever its source, truth is of the Holy Spirit.'

84 Humility

The New Testament repeatedly advocates humility. Firstly, it points to Jesus as the One who was 'gentle and humble in heart' (Mt 11:29). Secondly, Jesus spoke about the importance of humility: 'Everyone,' he said, 'who exalts himself will be humbled, and he who humbles himself will be exalted' (Lk 14:11). Later, the apostles repeatedly highlighted the importance of humility in the Christian life. For instance, in 1 Pet 5:5-6 we read: 'All of you, clothe yourselves with humility toward one another, because, God opposes the proud but gives grace to the humble. Humble yourselves, therefore, under God's mighty hand, that he may lift you up in due time.'

Pride is the opposite to humility. In the Greek of the New Testament it means 'above' in the sense of arrogantly and disdainfully putting oneself in a superior position. The Pharisees epitomised this attitude. Proud people, like them, are preoccupied with their reputations and status. They draw attention, often in boastful ways, to such things as their merits, possessions, qualifications and achievements. They like to be noticed, applauded and honoured. They can get very angry if their self-importance and reputations are threatened in any way as a result of being corrected, criticised or overlooked. Although they may appear to be well-mannered, proud people tend to be self-centred and hypocritical. Often outward appearances are used to hide shameful secrets, to do with such things as financial and sexual misdemeanors.

In the Greek of the New Testament the word for humility means 'of low degree, to be brought low'. With this in mind, it is interesting to note that the English word 'humility' comes the Latin *humus* meaning 'the ground'. Humble people, metaphorically bow towards the earth when they acknowledge that their natural and supernatural gifts come from God. They do not deny them. As Sir 10:27-28 says: 'My child, with humility have self-esteem; prize yourself as you deserve. Who will acquit the one who engages in self-condemnation? Who will honour the one who discredits him or herself?' When they boast, they boast in the Lord (cf 1 Cor 1:31). Humble people, however, are also realistic about their shortcomings. In the words of step four of Alcoholics Anonymous, they admit their failings to themselves, to God and to a chosen confidant such as a priest in confession.

Biblical humility is also manifested in people's attitude to others. As Paul wrote: 'Do nothing out of selfish ambition or vain conceit, but in humility consider others better than yourselves' (Phil 2:3). What does Paul means here? Like Jesus, who wrapped a towel around his waist before washing the feet of his disciples, humble people focus primarily on the satisfaction of the needs of others, in a spirit of service. They are also modest. They are more concerned with the glory of God than their own glory. They don't get too upset when they are corrected, overlooked or even humiliated. This is so because, as a result of their relationship with Jesus, their deepest desire is to imitate him by sharing in his humility, and if needs be, in his humiliations.

Pope John Paul I once wisely observed: 'I run the risk of making a blunder but I will say it: The Lord loves humility so much that sometimes he allows serious sins. Why? In order that those who committed them may, after repenting, remain humble. One does not feel inclined to think oneself half a saint, half an angel, when one knows that one has committed serious faults.' When asked how one might obtain humility, one father of the church replied: 'By keeping your eyes off other people's faults and fixing them on your own.'

85 Healing

In spite of its frequent breakthroughs, modern medicine is unable to cure many ailments of mind or body. As suffering people discover this, it is not surprising that they not only turn to alternative forms of therapy such as acupuncture, homeopathy, and reflexology, they sometimes resort to some of the stranger forms of New Age healing in the hope that they will bring them relief. It is really regrettable that quite often the ministry of Christian healing is overlooked.

Jesus wasn't content with preaching the good news of God's unconditional and unrestricted love for people, especially the poor and needy, he demonstrated that love by healing people of their physical and psycho-spiritual ailments. As St Peter said after the resurrection: 'You know what has happened throughout Judea, beginning in Galilee after the baptism that John preached – how God anointed Jesus of Nazareth with the Holy Spirit and power, and how he went around doing good and healing all who were under the power of the devil, because God was with him' (Acts 10:37-38).

Jesus commissioned his disciples to heal. For example in Lk 9:1-3 we read: 'Jesus called the twelve disciples together and gave them the power and the authority to cast out all demons and to cure diseases. Then he sent them to preach the kingdom of God and to heal the sick.' Before his ascension into heaven we are told in Mk 16:17-19: 'Believers will be given the power to perform miracles, they will drive out demons in my name; they will speak in strange tongues; if they pick up snakes or drink any poison they will not be harmed; they will place their hands on sick people who will get well.' We know that in the New Testament church the apostles healed many sick people. For example, in Acts 28:8 we read that Paul healed the father of Publius. 'When this had happened,' we are told in the following verse, 'the rest of the sick on the island came and were cured.'

Christ continues to offer salvation and healing to the church of our day. They are two sides of the same coin of God's love. Healing can be experienced as a result of:

1. Prayers of petition and intercession for healing.

2. The administration of the sacraments, especially the Eucharist, reconciliation and the anointing of the sick

3. Visiting shrines such as Lourdes and Knock.

4. Being blessed by a holy relic such as a glove of St Padre Pio.

5. The gift of unhesitating, expectant faith expressed by means of the laying on of hands, or anointing with oil. (cf Mk 16:14; 1 Cor 12:9) The Congregation of the Doctrine of the Faith published an *Instruction on Prayers for Healing* in 2000. It endorsed the fact that healing can and does occur in the church today. Article one of its disciplinary norms reads: 'It is licit for every member of the faithful to pray to God for healing. When this is organised in a church or other sacred place, it is appropriate that such prayers be led by an or-dained minister.'

Happily, many healings are being reported. I heard a few days ago, how a woman of faith, who works in a beauty salon, prayed for a client who had been suffering from a painful stomach complaint for about sixteen years. It cleared up completely. I know another woman who prayed for a Traveller boy who was in caliper splints because his legs were suffering from a congenital bone disease. Although doctors had said he was incurable, he recovered completely afterwards. Clearly, the healing ministry of Jesus continues in the contemporary church.

86 Suffering and Healing

I have conducted many healing services. I usually read one or two appropriate passages from the scriptures, in the belief that they can evoke firm faith in those who listen attentively in them (cf Rom 10:17). Then I give a homily which tries to do two things. Firstly, I stress the fact that God can, and sometimes does heal those who are ill in mind or body. In this section of the sermon, I comment on texts such as, 'whatever you ask in prayer, believe that you have received it, and it will be yours' (Mk 11:24); 'He called to him his twelve disciples and gave them authority ... to heal every disease and every infirmity' (Mt 10:1); and 'Is any among you sick? Let him call for the elders of the church, and let them pray over him, anointing him with oil in the name of the Lord; and the prayer of faith will save the sick man, and the Lord will raise him up ... pray for one another, that they may be healed' (Jas 5:14-16).

I also stress the fact that we need to pray for healing in accordance with God's will. It can be revealed by means of a reading that leaps alive off the page into the heart with an associated assurance that it is about to be fulfilled. The Lord's will can also be revealed by means of an intuition or inner conviction that is hard to explain in rational terms. If people are aware that they are praying in harmony with God's revealed purposes they can say: 'This is the confidence we have in approaching God: that if we ask anything according to his will, he hears us. And if we know that he hears us – whatever we ask – we know that we have what we asked of him' (1 Jn 5:14-15). At this point in a healing service I usually describe modern day examples of how the Lord has healed people as a result of prayers offered with expectant, unhesitating faith.

In the second part of the homily, I point out that the Lord doesn't always reveal the divine will to us. In those cases we can't be clear about God's purposes in the particular circumstances we find ourselves. I refer to the fact that although suffering is evil in itself, God the Father can allow it, as he did in Christ's life, for a redemptive purpose. As Pope John Paul II said in Knock: 'By your suffering you help Jesus in his work of salvation. This great truth is difficult to express accurately, but St Paul puts it this way: 'In my flesh I complete what is lacking in Christ's afflictions, for the sake of his body, that is, the church' (Col 1:24). I might also mention that Paul believed that suffering patiently borne could help people to grow in Christian virtues such as perseverance and compassion (cf Rom 5:3-5; 2 Cor 1:4). Having made points like these, I refer to the example of Christians whose lives have borne joyful witness to these mysterious truths.

Surely, these two points were succinctly, and poignantly expressed by Jesus when he prayed: 'Abba, Father, everything is possible for you. Take this cup from me. Yet not what I will, but what you will' (Mk 14:36). He had utter confidence in God's power to help. But in the absence of a revelation to do with the Father's intention to deliver him from suffering, he expressed a willingness to submit to whatever God allowed to happen to him, in the belief that evil would not have the last word. It would belong to God.

87 Simplicity

On one occasion the Pharisees said to Jesus: 'Master, we know that you are an honest man and teach the way of God in an honest way, and that you are not afraid of anyone, because a man's rank means nothing to you' (Mt 22:16). The Pharisees lacked simplicity. What they said was insincere and intended to flatter. Nevertheless they, unintentionally, testified to the truth. In doing so, they afforded us a fascinating glimpse into the simplicity of Jesus.

He was an utterly honest, God-intoxicated, person. When he spoke, he had a single-minded desire to bear witness to the presence, word and will of his loving Father. As a man of integrity he meant what he said, and said what he meant. He had no hidden agenda, or undeclared self-interest. Rather than being a people pleaser, his sole intention was to please God. He didn't want any kind of secret reward, such as popularity, influence or advantage.

Jesus neither ingratiated himself, in a sycophantic way, with the civil or religious authorities of his day, nor was he intimidated by their authority and power. As he said to Pilate: 'You would have no power over me unless it had been given you from God' (Jn 19:11). So Jesus didn't water down his message, either to make it more acceptable, or to ensure his personal safety. Like the prophets of old, he fearlessly and courageously spoke the truth. In doing so he indirectly signed his own death warrant.

Jesus saw everyone he met, from the highest to the lowest, as persons with equal dignity and worth. He said: 'You judge by human standards; I pass judgement on no one' (Jn 8:15). Years later, St James was to draw out one of the implications of this egalitarian perspective. 'My brothers and sisters,' he wrote, 'as believers in our glorious Lord Jesus Christ, don't show favouritism. Suppose a person comes into your meeting wearing a gold ring and fine clothes, and a poor person in shabby clothes also comes in. If you show special attention to the person wearing fine clothes and say, "Here's a good seat for you," but say to the poor person, "You stand there" or "Sit on the floor by

my feet," have you not discriminated among yourselves and become judges with evil thoughts?' (Jas 2:1-4).

Clearly, Jesus epitomised the virtue of simplicity. Speaking
about this quality St Vincent de Paul revealed that it was the
virtue he loved the most. 'God gives me such a great esteem for
simplicity,' he wrote, 'that I call it my gospel.' On another occasion he stated: 'Simplicity comprises more than the simple truth
and purity of intention. It puts far from us all deceit, trickery, or
duplicity. Since this virtue is shown chiefly in our words, we are
obliged to say exactly what is in our hearts with the pure intention of pleasing God alone. This is not to say that simplicity
obliges us to say everything in our mind. This virtue is discreet
and never opposed to prudence. It allows us to discern what
should or should not be said ... Just as this virtue requires us to
speak the way we think, it also makes us act with Christian
frankness and directness. All must be done for God and God
alone.'

Nowadays, simplicity is compromised by those whose apparently altruistic words and deeds are motivated by a disguised and self-serving desire for personal benefits, of one kind
or another. At a time when there are frequent examples of obfus-
cation, deceit and corruption, Christian transparency and au-
thenticity are much needed in the affairs of both church and
state.

88 Gentleness

For many people, especially men, the words gentle and gentleness conjure up images of a weak, whimpish, and unassertive person. Properly understood, however, gentleness is a very attractive Christian virtue. In classical Greek the word was *praus*. It could refer to mild things, such as a mellifluous voice; to taming animals, such as horses whose boisterous energies are controlled by bridle and bit; or to pleasant and agreeable men and women, such as those who never deliberately cause unnecessary pain. Aristotle though of gentleness as strength under control, the mid-point between extreme anger and apathetic indifference. In the New Testament, gentleness began to acquire added nuances of meaning. On the one hand, it was the first cousin of poverty of spirit, i.e. a sense of utter dependence on God, and on the other, it was also the first cousin of humility, i.e. an honest acknowledgement that ultimately all of one's gifts and graces come from God.

It is significant that Jesus said of himself that he was 'gentle and humble of heart' (Mt 11:29). He fulfilled the following prophecy in Mt 12:18-20: 'Here is my servant whom I have chosen ... He will not quarrel or cry out; no one will hear his voice in the streets. A bruised reed he will not break, and a smoldering wick he will not snuff out.' In his Beatitudes Jesus declared: 'Blessed are the gentle', i.e. those who are considerate, unassuming, and on good terms with God and their fellow human beings, 'for they shall inherit the earth' (Mt 5:5). The evangelists tell us that when Jesus entered Jerusalem in triumph on Palm Sunday scripture was fulfilled: 'See, your king comes to you, gentle and riding on a donkey, on a colt, the foal of a donkey.' The apostle to the Gentiles referred to gentleness as a fruit of the Spirit in Gal 5:23. He was so impressed by it that, on one occasion, he wrote: 'This is Paul himself appealing to you by the gentleness and patience of Christ' (2 Cor 10:1).

St Vincent de Paul believed that compassion and gentleness are inseparable. Compassion as empathy for someone who is suffering, needs to be expressed in a gentle and sensitive way

that takes account of his or her feelings and needs. St Francis de
Sales (1567-1622) was renowned for his gentleness. St Jane de
Chantal, his friend and confidant said of him: 'He looked gentle
and meek, there was gentleness in his eyes and voice and move-
ments, and he passed it on to the hearts of others. Gentleness he
used to say was the true spirit of the Christian. He once told me
that he had made this holy virtue his special aim for three years.'

If we desire to be gentle in our dealings with others, we must
first learn to be gentle with ourselves. St Francis de Sales wrote:
'We must not fret over our imperfections ... Bitterness against
ourselves springs from no other source than self-love, which is
disturbed and upset at seeing it's imperfections.' He added: 'We
must not fret over our own imperfections. Although reason requires that we must be displeased and sorry when we commit a
fault, we must refrain from bitter, gloomy, spiteful, and emotional displeasure. Many people are at fault in this way. When
overcome by anger they become angry at being angry, disturbed
at being disturbed, and vexed at being vexed.' Likewise we need
to be moderate and lenient when correcting others. As Francis
wisely observed: 'A spoonful of honey is better than a barrel of
vinegar.' Surely, a gentle and compassionate disposition reveals
something of the heart of Christ.

89 Praying For Others

Over the years many heartbroken people, principally parents, siblings and spouses have spoken to me about family members whose way of life was causing them to worry and to grieve. It might be a daughter who was living with a married man, a son who had a serious drink problem, a spouse who never prayed or went to church, a cousin who was prone to batter his wife. The concerned relative often feels powerless and guilty. They often blame themselves for not being able to do something constructive to prevent the problem. They frequently say to themselves, others and God, 'where did I go wrong?'

In cases like this, I usually refer them to a passage in the New Testament which stresses the importance of intercessory prayer. St John illustrates the potential efficacy of this kind of petition for others by saying it can bring about transformation in the lives of sinners. He writes in 1 Jn 5:16, 'If you see your brother or sister committing what is not a mortal sin, you will ask, and God will give life to such a one – to those whose sin is not mortal.' The reference, here, to mortal sin, is not to 'ordinary' grave sins but to some extremely deadly sin, such as the sin against the Holy Spirit or apostasy. The Johannine author is referring to prayer for a non-schismatic member of the community who has fallen into some kind of public sin, e.g. fraud or sexual impropriety. If members of the community pray with the kind of expectant faith already mentioned, St John promises that the prodigal person will eventually come to his or her senses, and repent.

John's teaching seems to be rooted in that of Jesus about the importance of persistence in intercessory prayer. He illustrated what he meant by such perseverance in two of his parables. Firstly there was the story of the friend who comes at midnight and continues to ask for bread until the householder gives it to him (cf Lk 11:5-9). Secondly there is the account of the importunate widow who keeps pestering the unjust judge who eventually gives her what she wants in order to get her off his back (cf Lk 18:2-9). So in effect Jesus is saying, keep on asking and you shall receive.

There are a number of well known examples of this kind of persevering and persistent prayer on behalf of those who have fallen repeatedly on the banana skin of their weakness. For instance, in his *Confessions*, Augustine tells us that, for many years, Monica, his mother, prayed for his conversion. He says that at one point she had a prophetic dream which assured her that her wayward son would eventually turn away from his old way of life and ask for baptism. He says: 'All this time, this chaste, devout and prudent woman, a widow such as is close to your heart, never ceased to pray at all hours and to offer you the tears she shed for me. The dream had given her new spirit and hope, but she gave no rest to her sighs and tears.' Nine years after the dream Monica's prayers were finally answered when Augustine was baptised by St Ambrose of Milan.

So if you are worried about the welfare of someone you love, keep the promises of scripture in mind, especially the one in 1 Jn 5:16. Then pray with persistence and perseverance for him or for her, in the confident expectation, that sooner or later – it may even be after your death – your prayers will be heard in whatever way the Lord thinks is best.

90 People Pleasers

St Paul testified on one occasion: 'I try to please all men in every-thing I do, not seeking my own advantage, but that of many, that they may be saved. Be imitators of me, as I am of Christ' (1 Cor 10:33-11:1). That sentiment was re-echoed when he wrote: 'We who are strong ought to put up with the failings of the weak, and not to please ourselves. Each of us must please our neighbour for the good purpose of building up the neighbour. For Christ did not please himself' (Rom 15:1-3). A number of points can be made here.

Firstly, when St Paul said that he was a people-pleaser what did he mean? The words 'to please' in the Greek New Testament implies that the person seeks the happiness of others by taking their opinions, desires, and interests into account. To please them in this sense is to carry out the golden rule of doing to others what you would like them to do to you (cf Mt 7:12; Lk 6:31).

Secondly, Paul says that to imitate him was tantamount to imitating his role model, Jesus Christ. The Lord lived to please others. As he said himself, 'The Son of Man came not to be served but to serve' (Mk 10:45). He gave eloquent expression to this propensity when he wrapped a towel around his waist and washed the feel of the disciples (cf Jn 13:1-17). There is a striking instance of this willingness to please others, by means of self-for-getful service, in the account of the people who went into the wilderness to search for Jesus. Although he himself was looking forward to some much needed rest and recreation after the exer-tions of his public ministry, Jesus put his own needs on hold in order to minister to those who looked 'sad and dejected like sheep without a shepherd' (Mk 6:34). He did this without a hint of frustration or recrimination.

Thirdly, St Paul suggested in a number of places how one could go about pleasing others in a similar, healthy-minded, Christian way. In Phil 2:3-5 he said: 'Do nothing from selfish am-bition or conceit, but in humility regard others as better than yourselves. Let each of you look not to your own interests, but to the interests of others. Let the same mind be in you that was in

Christ Jesus.' Again in 1 Cor 10:34 he explained: 'No one should seek his own advantage, but that of his neighbour.'

There is also a neurotic form of people-pleasing which St Paul did not favour. It is rooted in a lack of self-esteem and self-acceptance. It can be traced back to the experience of conditional loving in childhood, the kind that says, either verbally or non-verbally: 'I will love you more if … if you behave … if you do as your told … if you are successful.' Consequently, such children form the mistaken impression that their value and worth are dependant on what they do, and not upon who they are. As a result they seek to curry favour and to win brownie points by trying to please others in obsequious and sycophantic ways. They find it very hard to say 'no' lest others should think badly of them. They may be praised for being generous and kind, but in reality their apparent altruism is rooted in disguised self-interest. St Paul had this pseudo-love in mind when he wrote: 'Am I now seeking human approval, or God's approval? Or am I trying to please people? If I were still pleasing people, I would not be a servant of Christ' (Gal 1:10).

91 The Baptism of Jesus

The baptism of Jesus is the first of the new mysteries of light, which have been added to the rosary by John Paul II. It is appropriate because it was crucially important in the life of the One who is 'the light of the world' (Jn 8:12). In Mk 1:11, we are told: 'A voice came from heaven: "You are my Son, whom I love; with you I am well pleased."' These words were drawn from two texts in the Old Testament. In Is 42:1 the Lord said: 'Here is my servant, whom I uphold, my chosen one in whom I delight; I will put my Spirit on him.' Again in Ps 2:7 we read: 'He said to me, "You are my Son; today I have become your Father."' When he heard these words, Jesus realised a number of things.

Firstly, he became more consciously aware of the Father's infinite love for him as the Son of God endowed with every perfection of divinity. Pope Paul VI observed in part three of his encyclical *On Christian Joy*: 'Jesus ... knows that he is loved by his Father. When he is baptised on the banks of the Jordan, this love, which is present from the first moment of his incarnation, is manifested ... This certitude is inseparable from the consciousness of Jesus. It is a presence which never leaves him all alone ... For Jesus it is not a question of a passing awareness. It is the reverberation in his human consciousness of the love that he has always known as God in the bosom of the Father.' This awareness found its quintessential expression in the address, 'Abba, Father.'

Secondly, at his baptism, Jesus recognised that he was the promised Messiah. The people were expecting a political liberator who would begin by ridding them of the cruel yoke of Roman rule before going on to spread God's sovereignty throughout the world. But at the moment of his anointing by the Spirit, Jesus realised that his vocation was to be the suffering servant referred to by the prophet Isaiah. So although his baptism was a time of ecstatic happiness, there were already intimations of the cross to come. As the suffering servant Jesus would eventually be 'despised and rejected by men; a man of sorrows, and acquainted with grief' (Is 53:3).

203

Thirdly, as a result of his baptismal experience, Jesus became aware of his mission. He expressed it clearly in his local synagogue, in Nazareth, when he read these words: 'The Spirit of the Lord is on me, because he has anointed me to preach good news to the poor. He has sent me to proclaim freedom for the prisoners and recovery of sight for the blind, to release the oppressed, to proclaim the year of the Lord's favor' (Lk 4:18-19). As the evangeliser of the poor he was called to show to others, especially those who were 'sad and dejected like sheep without a shepherd' (Mt 9:36), the same unconditional and unrestricted love that God was showering on him. God wanted all his words and actions to be rooted in that love, to express that love and to foster that same love among those who believed in him.

Jesus was completely faithful to his baptismal identity and mission. Years later, St Peter was able to say of him: 'You know what has happened throughout Judea, beginning in Galilee after the baptism that John preached – how God anointed Jesus of Nazareth with the Holy Spirit and power, and how he went around doing good and healing all who were under the power of the devil, because God was with him' (Acts 10:37-38).

92 The Marriage Feast of Cana

The second of the mysteries of light is the story of Mary's intercession at the marriage feast of Cana (Jn 2:1-11). The roots of her
role as gracious advocate are to be found in the Old Testament.
At one time in Israel the king could have many wives. In order
to avoid rivalries and disputes, the queen mother was honoured
as the first lady in the land. She was referred to as the 'great
lady'. She assisted the king in ruling the kingdom and had two
interrelated roles. Firstly, she was the king's counsellor. She
would advise him about administrative matters. Secondly, she
had the role of advocate. The ordinary people could approach
her with their requests, and she would present them to her son,
the king.

There is an instructive example of what was involved in 1
Kgs 2:19-20. It is about the relationship that existed between
King Solomon and his mother Bathsheba. In the text we are told
that on a state occasion, 'The king rose to meet her, and bowed
down to her; and he sat on his throne, and had a seat brought for
the king's mother, and she sat on his right. Then she said, "I
have one small request to make of you, do not refuse me." And
the king said to her, "make your request, my mother, for I will
not refuse you."'

There is a similar story in Esther chapters 7-8. Like Bathsheba,
queen Esther had great influence over the king. On one occasion
he said to her. 'What is your petition, Queen Esther? It shall be
granted you. And what is your request? Even to half of my kingdom it shall be fulfilled' (Esth 7:2). The Queen begged king
Ahasuererus to put an end to the evil plan of Haman who intended killing the queen's fellow Jews. We are told that the king
granted her request, sentenced Haman to death, and gave Esther
his authority to write to the people on his behalf. He said: 'Now
write another decree in the king's name in behalf of the Jews as
seems best to you, and seal it with the king's signet ring – for no
document written in the king's name and sealed with his ring
can be revoked' (Esth 8:3-8).

During the marriage feast of Cana, Mary noticed that the

wine was running short. Wishing to prevent embarrassment,
she interceded with a confidence greater than that of queens
Bathsheba and Esther. We are told that 'When the wine failed
the mother of Jesus said to him. "They have no wine." And Jesus
said to her, "O woman, what have you to do with me? My hour
has not come yet."' Although Jesus had received the ability to
perform deeds of power at his baptism, clearly he didn't feel authorised to exercise it. As he acknowledged on one occasion:
'The Son can do only what he sees the Father doing; and whatever
the Father does, the Son does too' (Jn 5:19). Nevertheless, Mary
said to the servants, 'Do whatever he tells you.' Although, up to
that moment, Jesus had no reason to believe that the Father desired him to perform a deed of power, he discerned in his mother's request that the hour had finally arrived. He recognised that
her spontaneous impulse of loving concern and firm confidence
in his powers were inspired by the Spirit and therefore an expression of the Father's will. Just as she had given birth to Jesus
as a result of her obedient faith at the annunciation, so now she
was giving birth to his public ministry, as a result of the same
docile trust.

93 Proclamation of the Kingdom and Conversion

The proclamation of the kingdom was the central message in Christ's preaching and teaching. It is surprising, therefore, that he never defined what he meant by the term. Instead he used everyday images such as seeds, yeast, treasure, pearls, and nets to convey his understanding of this mystery. It would probably be true to say that, in all of them, Jesus was proclaiming the possibility of divinisation as a result of conversion and justification by divine grace. As St Paul was to declare a few years after the death and resurrection of Jesus: 'The kingdom of God is not a matter of eating and drinking, but of righteousness, peace and joy in the Holy Spirit' (Rom 14:17).

Jesus began his public ministry with the announcement that 'the kingdom of God is near. Repent and believe the Good News!' (Mk 1:5). 'You are sinners who have been influenced by the spirit of evil. But you have no need to be afraid of God's justice or punishments. Though very real, they are on hold, so to speak, until the day of judgement. Meantime you are living in the age of God's unrestricted and unconditional mercy. So if you acknowledge your shortcomings with a sorrowful purpose of amendment and look only into the eyes of God's mercy, expecting only mercy, you will receive only mercy, now and at the hour of your death.'

Jesus demonstrated the benign rule of the Lord in a number of ways. Firstly, he believed that God's kingdom was in conflict with the kingdom of Satan, the malign ruler of this world (cf Jn 12:31; Lk 8:26-39). He demonstrated the in-breaking of God's liberating power by means of the exorcisms he performed. As he said on one occasion: 'If I cast out devils by the finger of God, then the kingdom of God has come upon you' (Lk 11:20). Secondly, Jesus healed the sick and took action to free the people from the socio-political evils that oppressed them. These were further signs that God's reign was being established in a benevolent way.

Jesus was sent to preach the good news of the kingdom to the poor (cf Lk 4:18), i.e. those who, like children, would accept it with humble hearts. As he said: 'Who is the greatest in the kingdom of heaven?' And calling to him a child, he put him in the midst of them, and said, 'Truly I say to you, unless you turn and become like children, you will never enter the kingdom of heaven.' Commenting on this verse St Thérèse of Lisieux wrote: 'To be a child is to recognise our nothingness, to expect everything from God as a little child expects everything from its father; it is to be disquieted about nothing.' In adult life, childlike reliance on God is expressed by following the providential plan of God in the belief that all our other needs, whether material or spiritual will be taken care of (cf Lk 12:31).

While the church is a manifestation of the kingdom, it is not confined to it. It is also present among sincere people, whether members of other religions or not, who have received baptism of desire in virtue of seeking the truth and obeying the dictates of their consciences (cf *Catechism of the Catholic Church*, pars 1258, 1260, 1281). Finally, there is something paradoxical about the reign of God. On the one hand it is already present. As Jesus said: 'The kingdom of God is among you' (Lk 17:20-21), while on the other hand it will not be completely established until the second coming. That is why we say in the Lord's Prayer, 'Thy kingdom come' (Mt 6:10).

94 The Transfiguration

A number of years ago I read a book by Maurice Bucke, entitled *Cosmic Consciousness*. It maintained that most of the world's great religious leaders had life transforming mystical experiences. For example, when St John of the Cross was enlightened by God during a time when he was in jail, he was literally radiant as a result. One biography states that: 'One night the man who was on guard went as usual to see that his prisoner was safe and witnessed the heavenly light with which his cell was flooded.' Bucke suggested that something similar occurred following the baptism and transfiguration of Jesus. These were interrelated events, the one subjective and private, the other objective and public, when the light of Christ's inner illumination burst forth in the form of his external glory.

We are told that Moses, the archetypal lawgiver, and Elijah, the outstanding prophet of the Old Testament, were talking to Jesus. Their differing contributions found fulfillment in the person of the Messiah. Then 'a cloud appeared and enveloped them, and they were afraid as they entered the cloud' (Lk 9:34). This image has scriptural roots. It is a reminder of the time, on Mount Sinai, when God spoke to Moses from a cloud. It is also reminiscent of the occasions when Moses went into the tent of meeting. When it was overshadowed by the cloud of God's presence he would converse with the Lord face to face (cf Ex 33:11).

Mystics have pointed out that, at first, the apostles could see and hear Christ. But as the experience deepened, a metaphorical cloud of unknowing enveloped them. As a result, although they could no longer see and hear Jesus, they knew in faith that he was present. Likewise, as Christians mature in the spiritual life they are often weaned off ideas and images of the divine. Then they have to be content to let their wills, if not their minds and imaginations, rest in the incomprehensible mystery of the One who 'dwells in unapproachable light' (1 Tim 6:16).

In the gospels we are told that 'a voice from the cloud said, "This is my Son, whom I love; with him I am well pleased"' (Mt

17:5). You will notice that these were the same words that were spoken when God addressed Jesus at his baptism. Now the disciples had first-hand knowledge of the fact that, although the Father was lavishing unimaginable love on his only begotten Son, he was destined, nevertheless, to suffer and die in Jerusalem. The preface of the Mass of the transfiguration explains succinctly: 'He revealed his glory to the disciples to strengthen them for the scandal of the cross.'

It is highly significant that the words, 'Listen to him' (Mk 9:7), is one of the few recorded instances of the Father talking to humanity. We can listen to the words of Jesus in a number of ways. He can speak to us through his teachings in the scriptures, through his inspirations in prayer, and through people who are inspired by his Holy Spirit. Jesus stated: 'If anyone loves me, he will keep my word. My Father will love him, and we will come to him and make our home with him' (Jn 14:23).

The transfiguration is a Trinitarian incident: the Father is the voice, the Son is the man, the Spirit is the shining cloud. Finally, there are intimations of the definitive coming of the kingdom at the end of time in the transfiguration. The fact that Christ's glory shone forth from a body like our own, shows that the church, which is the body of Christ, will one day share his glory.

95 The Eucharist

The institution of the Eucharist commemorates the saving death and resurrection of Jesus, mysteries which were foreshadowed in his baptism and transfiguration. The marriage feast of Cana also pointed to the Eucharist. Instead of water being changed into wine, God's glory is manifested each time wine is changed into the body, blood, soul and divinity of Christ. When Jesus proclaimed the coming of the kingdom, he had God's definitive victory in mind, when love would triumph, at the end of time, over every obstacle. This fact will be celebrated at the great eucharistic banquet of heaven.

There are many scriptural texts we could examine. However, I have opted to look at the account of the disciples meeting with Jesus on the road to Emmaus (Lk 24:13-35). As Pope John Paul observes in *Ecclesia de Eucharistia*: 'The Eucharist is ... a mystery of light. Whenever the church celebrates the Eucharist, the faithful can in some way relive the experience of the two disciples on the road to Emmaus: "Their eyes were opened and they recognised him" (Lk 24:31).'

Although he was an evangelist, Luke was never an apostle. Because he hadn't met the Lord in person, he had to answer the question, 'How do those of us who live in the post-resurrection era come to know the Lord?' His account of the meeting of Jesus with the disciples on the road is his answer. What Luke is saying is that believers meet the risen Jesus in and through the eucharistic community. When one examines the text closely it becomes apparent that it has a liturgical structure.

Firstly, there is the gathering of the faithful, represented by the two disciples, who share common life experiences. They are clearly, troubled, disillusioned, and walking away from Jerusalem the city of their broken dreams. Then they are joined by a mysterious stranger. In reality it was Jesus, but they didn't recognise him. While this encounter may have had an historical basis, it certainly has a symbolic significance because Jesus had promised: 'Where two or three meet in my name, there am I am there among them' (Mt 18:20).

Secondly, the two disciples share their feelings with the stranger. They tell him about the tragic death of the Messiah, the one on whom they had pinned all their hopes. Then they listened to the liturgy of the word, when relevant scripture texts were recalled and explained by the stranger. Luke tells us that: 'beginning with Moses and all the prophets he explained to them what was said in all the scriptures concerning himself' (Lk 24:27). Hearing the inspired readings and homily had a profound effect upon the two men. They later remarked: 'Were not our hearts burning within us while he talked with us on the road and opened the scriptures to us?' (Lk 24:32).

Thirdly, the story reaches its climax when the two disciples reach their destination. They invite their travelling companion to join them. The evangelist tells us what happened: 'When he was at the table with them, he took bread, gave thanks, broke it and began to give it to them. Then their eyes were opened and they recognised him, and he disappeared from their sight' (Lk 24:30-31). Christ is really and truly present in the eucharistic community where grateful thanks is offered through the Lord for the loving and redemptive sacrifice he has offered on its behalf.

I heard a memorable prophecy once which said: 'My people, unless you discern my presence in the scriptures and in one another, especially the poor and needy among you, you will not be able to discern my presence in the breaking of bread.'

96 The Advent of Christ

There is a wonderful text in the Old Testament which I always associate with Christmas. In Wis 18:14-15 we read: 'For when peaceful stillness compassed everything and the night in its swift course was half spent, your all-powerful word from heaven's royal throne bounded, a fierce warrior, into the doomed land, bearing the sharp sword of your inexorable decree.' When one ponders these verses it becomes immediately obvious why the church associates them with the birth of Jesus Christ over 2000 years ago. But it has often occurred to me when I pondered these inspired words that they also described the way in which we become aware of the coming of, and indwelling of Christ in our hearts.

God comes to us in silence. However, speaking of modern culture, poet T. S. Eliot wrote in *Choruses From the Rock*: 'The endless cycle of idea and action, endless invention, endless experiment, brings knowledge of motion, but not of stillness; knowledge of speech, but not of silence; knowledge of words, and ignorance of the Word.' It is true. We live in the age of noise, physical noise, mental noise and the noise of disordered desire for such things as power, pleasure, popularity, and possessions. No wonder the psalmist says: 'Be still before the Lord and wait patiently for him' (Ps 37:7). St John of the Cross explained the reason why: 'The Father uttered one Word; that Word is his Son, and he utters him forever in everlasting silence; and in silence the soul has to hear it.' We need to stop our activities, to relax our stressful bodies, and to calm our agitated minds and hearts. We do this in order to listen to the gentle whisper of our own inner desire for the infinite, for God.

God can come to us in darkness. The lack of light is a symbol for desolation of spirit; the absence of felt sense of the presence of God. Speaking about this state, St Ignatius of Loyola explained: 'The term spiritual desolation describes our interior life when we find ourselves enmeshed in a certain turmoil of spirit or feel ourselves weighed down by a heavy darkness or weight.' Ignatius also said that the Lord may withdraw consolation from the soul as a result of spiritual laziness, neglect of prayer, or lack of real effort in resisting temptation and sin. Whenever we have to endure a sort of dark night of the soul, we begin to yearn in a more wholehearted way for the Lord. Wisdom 18:15 assures us that just when it seems that the divine presence has been totally eclipsed, God's all powerful Word leaps from heaven's throne into the doomed land of the apparently, abandoned soul.

God comes principally by means of the sword of the word. When we are receptive to divine inspirations during times of inner silence and darkness, the Lord can come to us by means of a revelatory word of scripture which jumps alive off the page, crackling with relevance and meaning. As Heb 4:12 observes: 'The word of God is living and effective, sharper than any two-edged sword, penetrating even between the soul and spirit, joints and marrow, and able to discern reflections and thoughts of the heart.' As a result of receiving the word with the obedience of faith, Christ comes to live within the inner self, in a new way (cf Eph 3:17). As St Paul testified in 2 Cor 4:6, 'For God said, "Let light shine out in darkness," has shone in our hearts to bring to light the knowledge of the glory of God on the face of Jesus Christ.'

97 Remember, Repent, and Act

Like modern Christianity, early Christianity was largely an urban affair. Take Ephesus for example. It was a large city with a multi-racial population of over 250,000 people. They had a reputation for superstition, immorality and wealth. Ephesus was pagan and had the greatest temple in the world, dedicated to the goddess Artemis. In a number of respects Ephesus was quite similar to many modern cities.

Paul visited Ephesus around 52 AD. He remained there for more than two years. During that time he founded a thriving Christian community. As you know, the New Testament includes Paul's epistle to the Ephesians. Some thirty years later, St John addressed another inspired letter to the same church. It is to be found in Rev 2:2-7. Part of it reads: 'I know your deeds, your hard work and your perseverance. I know that you cannot tolerate wicked men, that you have tested those who claim to be apostles but are not, and have found them false. You have persevered and have endured hardships for my name, and have not grown weary. Yet I hold this against you: You have forsaken your first love. Remember the height from which you have fallen! Repent and do the things you did at first.'

When you read the letter closely you will notice that it has three main parts, one of commendation, another of condemnation and the third of recommendation. In the commendatory section, John begins by congratulating the community for its faithfulness. They have resisted false doctrines, endured their trials and tribulations with patience, and rejected the permissive moral standards prevailing at the time. In the condemnatory section, however, John reproaches the community for losing the enthusiasm with which its members had first embraced the gospel of loving mercy. Although they are still persevering in the faith they lack their initial zest and zeal. In the final section of his letter, John recommends that the Ephesian Christians do three things, to remember, repent and act.

Firstly, they should begin by remembering their first fervour which filled them with 'an inexpressible and glorious joy' (1 Pet

1:8). Secondly, they should go on to repent by turning away from anything that would involve compromise or mediocrity. Speaking about this, the Lord says in Rev 3:15; 19-20: 'I know your deeds, that you are neither cold nor hot. I wish you were either one or the other … be earnest, and repent. Here I am! I stand at the door and knock.' Thirdly, when they come to their senses, John recommends that the Christian community should go on to act in a more wholehearted and conscientious way.

It has occurred to me, that these verses are still relevant for many members of the contemporary church, especially middle-aged Christians who, in spite of remaining faithful, can become spiritually stale and complacent. Medieval writers referred to this apathetic tendency as 'accidie,' or the noon-day devil of laziness and discouragement. Such people are reluctant to leave their comfort zones. Consciously or unconsciously they tend to take the line of least resistance while espousing the adage, 'the devil you know is better than the devil you don't know.'

What should they do? In words that echo those of St John, Jeremiah advises: 'Halt at the crossroads, look well, and ask yourselves which path it was that stood you in good stead long ago. That path follow, and you will find rest for your souls' (Jer 6:16). When you recall your first fervour, try also to sense the intensity and purity of desire that led you to take your current Christian path. It is the God-given springboard to future growth.

98 Holy Fear

The Bible says in a number of places: 'The fear of the Lord is the beginning of wisdom' (Prov 9:10; Job 28:28; Ps 111:10; Sir 1:16). Those who have a forbidding image of God, either because of a puritanical upbringing or intimidating experiences of authority figures in childhood, tend to have a servile fear of the deity as someone who is remote and demanding. However, this is not what the inspired texts intend to say. The word 'fear' could be better understood if it was translated as 'reverential awe,' the kind of awareness that acknowledges the power and honour of some exalted person. So when people fear God, it means that they are expressing a fundamental religious attitude, as imperfect creatures, in the presence of the infinite perfection of their Creator. This kind of disposition is prompted by grace.

In the twentieth century a scholar called Otto wrote a well known book entitled, *The Idea of The Holy.* In it he maintained that when human beings have a genuine awareness of the divine, they experience it as a tremendous mystery, something that transcends their everyday perception and rational understanding. It usually has three interrelated characteristics.

Firstly, it so fills those who are aware of transcendent reality, with such a sense of dread that it virtually causes them to tremble. For instance, when the prophet Isaiah experienced the incomprehensible holiness of God in the temple, we are told that: 'The foundations of the threshold shook at the voice of him who called, and the house was filled with smoke. And I said: "Woe is me! For I am lost; for I am a man of unclean lips, … For I have seen the King the Lord of hosts!"' (Is 6:5). St Peter had a similar reaction when he witnessed the miraculous catch of fish. Aware of the otherworldly power of Jesus, he said: 'Depart from me, for I am a sinful man, O Lord' (Lk 5:8).

Secondly, awareness of the majesty of God is almost overpowering in its impact. Confronted with the omnipotence of the Lord, there is a sense of 'creature feeling' an emotion of awe as one humbly acknowledges one's absolute dependence on the Almighty for existence, moment by moment. As the psalmist says: 'What is man that you are mindful of him, and the son of man that you care for him? And yet you have made him little less than God.' Dame Julian of Norwich encapsulated this notion when she observed that the Lord sustains all things in being, including ourselves, and is therefore our Maker, Keeper and Lover.

Thirdly, there is a recognition of enormous energy being associated with the supernatural reality of the divine. This comes across in a number of biblical texts. For example, in Ex 3:2 we are told how Moses indirectly encountered God's presence in the form of a burning bush. Then in Ex 24:17 we are told: 'To the Israelites the glory of the Lord was seen as a consuming fire on the mountaintop.' Finally, Deut 4:24 states that: 'The Lord your God is a consuming fire.' Is it any wonder then, that when the Holy Spirit filled the disciples on Pentecost Sunday, it symbolically appeared as tongues of energising flame.

From a biblical point of view, reverence for God, and all that it implies, is the foundation stone of a truly religious disposition. It enables people not only to acknowledge the divine sovereignty, but also to obey God's commandments and to shun all forms of evil. As Ps 33:8 says: 'Let all the earth fear the Lord, let all the inhabitants of the world stand in awe of him.'

99 Awareness of Sin

Over the years, I have heard the confessions of thousands of people. It is surprising how many of them have little or no conscious awareness of sin. For example a young woman says, 'Bless me father, I think its about three years since my last confession.' I go on to ask, 'Have you offended God in any way during that time?' 'No,' she replies, 'not really Father.' I go on to inquire, 'Have you failed to love your neighbour in any way? For instance, have you said anything hurtful, broken a promise, or been jealous or envious in any way?' After a short pause she responds, 'Quite honestly, no! I get on well with everyone.' I find responses like these both discouraging and frustrating. While I can see that the penitent is sincere, she seems to be sadly lacking in realism.

I'm not sure why so many people are losing a sense of sin. It may be a matter of poor catechesis, presumption, immaturity, a lack of self-awareness, blaming psycho-social factors, or some other such cause. In spite of the contemporary denial of personal wrongdoing, the bible insists that it is a universal phenomenon. For example, in Rom 3:23 St Paul states: 'For all have sinned and fall short of the glory of God.' For his part, St John adds: 'If we claim we have not sinned, we make him out to be a liar and his word has no place in our lives' (1 Jn 1:10).

In the scriptures, awareness of sin is seen primarily as a gift of God rather than as a fruit of personal effort, e.g. by using a detailed examination of conscience. In Jer 17:9-10 we read: 'The heart is deceitful above all things and beyond cure. Who can understand it? I the Lord search the heart and examine the mind, to reward a man according to his conduct, according to what his deeds deserve.' In Wis 12:2 we read: 'You correct little by little those who trespass, and you remind and warn them of the things through which they sin, so that they may be freed from wickedness.' Mindful of this, the psalmist prays: 'Test me, O Lord, and try me, examine my heart and my mind' (Ps 26:2), and again, 'Search me, O God, and know my heart; test me and know my anxious thoughts. See if there is any offensive way in me' (Ps 139:23-24). In the sacrament of reconciliation, the priest echoes these sentiments when he prays, 'May the Lord who enlightens every heart, enlighten yours to know your sins and to trust in his mercy.'

Some time ago when I was reading the greatest of all the penitential psalms, I was particularly struck by the words: 'For I know my transgressions, and my sin is always before me. Against you, you only, have I sinned *and done what is evil in your sight* (my italics)' (Ps 51:3-4). Nowadays, many people are inclined to see sin in individualistic, self-serving, subjective terms, as that which is evil in *their* sight. Consequently, they tend to minimise and excuse its seriousness. But the scriptures see sin in a more objective manner as that which is evil in God's sight. It is only when we are consciously aware of God, and the loving ways of God, mainly by means of prayerful reflection on scripture, that we will honestly acknowledge how we have failed. But as Ps 130:3-4 says, 'If you, O Lord, should mark our guilt, who would survive? But with you is found forgiveness, and for this we revere you.'

100 Praying The Psalms

The bible is a library of books. It contains innumerable ideas, images and teachings. I was interested to see that scripture scholar, Albert Gelin, suggested in a book on the psalms that the whole Bible could be encapsulated in the following verses: 'Moses said to Yahweh, "Do let me see your glory!" Yahweh answered, "I will make all my goodness pass before you"' (Ex 33:18-19). There is a lot to be said for Gelin's contention.

The saints are agreed that the Christian life is first and foremost a matter of desire. St Augustine said: 'The whole life of a good Christian is a holy desire.' In other words, spirituality and prayer are fundamentally the expression of spiritual desires to experience God. St Thomas Aquinas explained: 'In prayer we simply express our desires to God. When I desire something, I ask for it by praying.' When we have a desire to know God's glory, i.e. the presence, word, will and assistance of God, scripture promises that it will be satisfied. For instance in Ps 10:17 we read: 'You hear, O Lord, the desire of the afflicted; you encourage them, and you listen to their cry,' and Ps 102:16-17 adds: 'For the Lord ... will respond to the prayer of the destitute; he will not despise their plea.'

The 150 psalms in the Old Testament, many of which were written by King David, comprise a unique anthology of prayers, poems and hymns, that express all kinds of human desires and feelings to God. They also acknowledge how God responded to them, time and time again. During periods of prayer we should tell the Lord the truth, the whole truth and nothing but the truth about our desires and emotions, no matter how negative they might be. That is what the psalmist did. He expressed what was in his heart, without editing or censoring it in any way. So these liturgical and personal psalms express the full gamut of our human experiences.

There are many categories of psalm. There are songs of thanksgiving, hymns of praise, protestations of repentance and confession, psalms which invoke evil upon enemies, messianic psalms, and songs sung by pilgrims as they travelled to

Jerusalem to observe one of the great festivals of their faith. When you pray the psalms you may notice that they sometimes contain intimations about the forthcoming person and work of Jesus Christ. For instance, Ps 23, 'The Lord is my Shepherd,' points to Jesus the good shepherd, while Ps 22:1 contains the words that Jesus would quote on the cross: 'My God, my God, why have you forsaken me?'

As you know, priests, religious and a growing number of lay people pray the Divine Office every day. The psalms take pride of place in each section. I must confess there are times when the words of particular psalms don't seem to be relevant because they fail to mirror the mood I'm in at that particular time. Many years ago I heard an expert liturgist observe that the psalms in the Divine Office were primarily intended to express the feelings and needs of the church rather than one's personal sentiments. I found that an extremely helpful remark. So if, for example, I'm in really good humour, I don't mind saying a psalm of lamentation. I recite it on behalf of fellow human beings who currently feel oppressed and without hope.

As par 2597 of the *Catechism of the Catholic Church* declares: 'Prayed and fulfilled in Christ, the psalms are an essential and permanent element of the prayer of the church. They are suitable for men and women of every condition and time.'

101 Maranatha: Come Lord Jesus

One of the Eucharistic acclamations says succinctly, 'Christ has died, Christ is risen, Christ will come again.' You will notice that it involves time past, present and future. Christ's saving death occurred 2000 years ago. The risen Lord is with us now through the sanctifying activity of the Holy Spirit. But then we look to the future, to the indeterminate time when Christ will return in glory to judge the living and the dead. The notion of the second coming or end-time has its roots in the gospels and the early church.

Biblical scholars tell us that Jesus had a strong sense that history was coming to an end and that the definitive intervention of God's liberating power was immanent. There are a number of other texts, which taken at face value, state that the end of history would occur soon after the resurrection and ascension of Jesus. For instance, in Mk 9:1 Jesus says: 'Truly, I assure you, there are some standing here who will not taste death before they see the kingdom of God come with power.' Christians often say the words of the Lord's prayer without realising that its petitions can only be properly understood as requests that focus on the second coming. To give just one example: the reference to 'daily bread' may refer, not only to the Eucharist, but also to the great banquet of heaven which will be celebrated when Christ comes again. So the petition 'Give us this day our daily bread' could justifiably be translated: 'Give us today a foretaste of the heavenly banquet to come.'

Clearly, the New Testament church was deeply influenced by this expectation of the immanence of the second coming. It is referred to on a number of occasions, especially in the earlier epistles of St Paul. For example, he says in 1 Thess 4:15: 'According to the Lord's own word, we tell you that we who are still alive, who are left till the coming of the Lord, will certainly not precede those who have fallen asleep.' However, as time passed, and the second coming did not take place, the early church began to suspect that it might be delayed for some time. In the interim, it had the duty of building up the kingdom of

God on earth. However, the church kept the end time in mind and prayed for its coming. For instance in 1 Cor 16:22 we read: 'If anyone does not love the Lord – a curse be on him. Maranatha!' The word *maranatha* is Aramaic and literally means 'come Lord Jesus,' a petition that asks the Lord to return in glory as a prelude to the definitive conquest of good over evil.

The *Catechism of the Catholic Church* warns in par 684-686: 'Before Christ's second coming the church must pass through a final trial that will shake the faith of many believers. The persecution that accompanies her pilgrimage on earth will unveil the "mystery of iniquity" in the form of a religious deception offering people an apparent solution to their problems at the price of apostasy from the truth. The supreme religious deception is that of the Antichrist, a pseudo-messianism by which man glorifies himself in place of God and of his Messiah come in the flesh … The church will enter the glory of the kingdom only through this final Passover, when she will follow her Lord in his death and resurrection. The kingdom will be fulfilled, then, not by an historic triumph of the church through a progressive ascendancy, but only by God's victory over the final unleashing of evil.' Nevertheless, we pray: 'So be it. Come Lord Jesus!' (Rev 22:20).